THE OXFORD CHILDREN'S HISTORY OF BRITAIN

THE
TUDORS &
STUARTS

Roy Burrell

CHANCELLOR
PRESS

First published in Great Britain in 1980 by
Oxford University Press under the series title
Oxford Junior History
by arrangement with the British Broadcasting
Corporation

This edition published in 1988 by
Chancellor Press
59 Grosvenor Street
London W1

© Roy Burrell 1980

ISBN 1 85152 075 9

Printed in Czechoslovakia
50681

Contents

Chapter One Tudor England

1 Henry VII

It is 1501, the first year of a new century. Let us walk through the fields from London to Westminster. There is a man sitting on a gate at the side of the road.

'Why are you looking so sad?' we ask.

Henry VII

'I shall lose my employment shortly and my fine uniform too,' he replies, 'and it's all the king's doing.' We ask him to explain.

'Well, King Henry VII has told all the great lords that they can no longer keep their private armies. He's also forbidden them to build castles without his permission. I can see why he's saying this. He still doesn't feel safe.'

'Why shouldn't the king feel safe?'

'For the last fifty years or so the great lords have been fighting each other to see who should be king. Fifteen years ago Henry won a great battle at Bosworth and took the throne.

He wants to stay on top. He keeps the lords weak so they can't make war on him. If they break his laws he brings them here to Westminster and tries them in his Court of Star Chamber. He makes them pay heavy fines. He even makes them pay fines if they've done nothing wrong!'

'*How can he do that?*'

'He calls the fines "loans", but they're not. My own master was forced to lend the king money. Many of the lords are so poor now that they just can't afford to keep paying wages to their soldiers. That's why I shall be out of work. I've no idea what I'm going to do. Soldiery is the only trade I know. I might even have to beg.' We wish him good luck and go on our way.

Henry VII wanted to make certain that the threats he faced when he became king did not grow into serious dangers. This is how he dealt with these threats:

| No castles · | Treaties by royal marriages | No private armies |

2 Printing

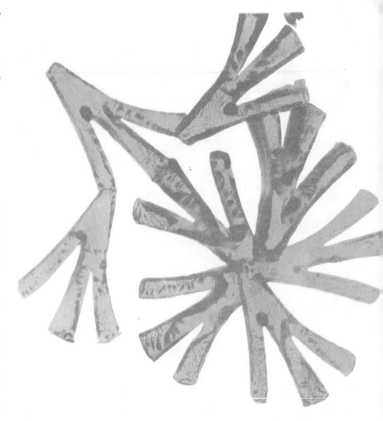

Have you ever made a potato print or a lino cut? It is easy to make shapes and patterns but if you want words or letters, you will have to cut them back to front. You might like to try and print your initials on your belongings.

People have known how to do this for thousands of years. In the picture below is an example of an Egyptian seal. It is like a little roller with picture words carved into it. If a man wanted to put his name on a wine jar, he would wrap a strip of soft clay over the neck and then roll his seal across it.

Roman potters stamped their names on their wares while the clay was still wet. There is an example on this page. It seems strange that no one at that time thought of printing books. The idea of doing so appeared in Europe and China round about the 1440s. Shortly afterwards, there were printers at work in both Germany and Holland.

William Caxton printed the first English book in England. He was a good reader but had grown tired of writing out the works he wanted to study. He was a rich London merchant whose business took him abroad from time to time.

He visited Bruges in what is now Belgium and saw the new invention of printing at work. He came back to England and set up his own press at Westminster in 1474. We call a printing works a press because the paper used to be pressed on to the type. Let's ask Wynkyn, the young man who works for Caxton, to explain.

'You have to make your own type,' he says. 'You start with some short rods of steel like these. You paint the letter you want on the end and then cut away the metal you don't want with a special chisel. Now there is a raised letter at the end of the rod. You can see that it's back to front.'

'Are they ready for printing?'

'Oh no! If you did that the letters wouldn't look alike. Printers who work with wooden types have found that out. Each time you carve a "B", for instance, it's slightly different.'

'What do you do then?'

'Well, you have to make a copper mould from each steel letter. Then you can pour hot lead into the moulds as many times as you like. Now all the "B"s, for example, will be identical. After trimming, they are ready. How many bits of type do you think we use?'

Printing

'All the letters of the alphabet: that's 26. Oh, and the numbers: that's another ten. Wait a minute — you'll need full stops, commas and things like that. About 40?'

'Look behind you,' he says. 'Every little wooden box has a different type in it and there are over two hundred boxes.'

'Why so many?' we ask.

'Because the letters on a page all have to be printed at once,' replies Wynkyn. 'If you wanted to set "these three trees" you'd need more than one of each letter. And the letters come in many different sizes.

'The printer puts the letters in his stick from right to left. He mustn't forget the spaces between words either. Then, a line at a time, he puts them into a frame and packs the blank areas with pieces of wood and wooden wedges. He taps the type gently all over with a small board and a mallet to make sure it is level. If it wasn't, not all the letters would show on the finished page.

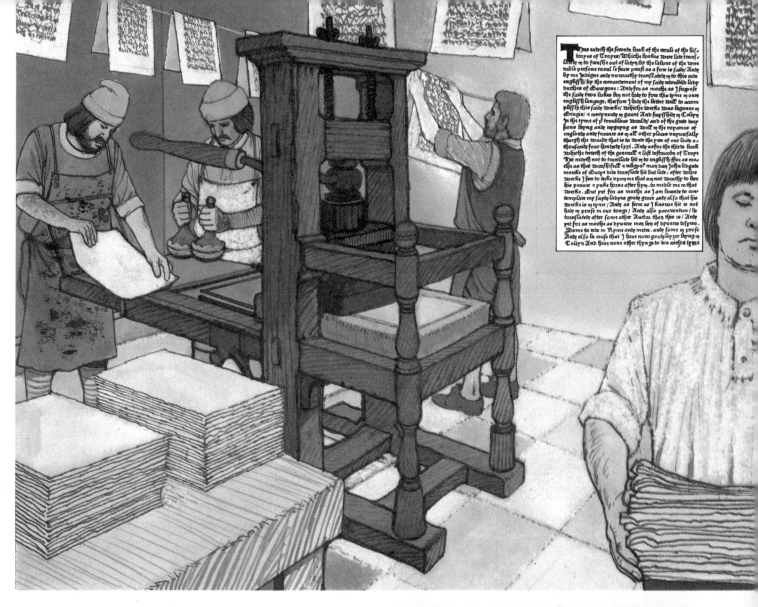

'Then he locks the type tight with the wedges and a man called a "devil" dabs inky pads all over the typeface. We lay the paper over it and a pad next to the paper. A board goes on top. The whole lot is fed into this machine and pressed together. Now the work is done.

'My master, William Caxton, has already printed *The Canterbury Tales* and a history of Troy. This is only a beginning, you wait and see. What will the world be like when books are cheap and everyone can read and write?'

Wynkyn was right. Oxford University Press, which publishes this book, was set up only a few years after Caxton's business was founded and celebrated its 500th anniversary in 1978.

3 Sir Thomas More

Thomas was born in Milk Street, London, on 7 February 1478, the son of a judge. He was a bright, merry boy who was always fond of a joke. He did well at school and went on to Canterbury College in Oxford. Later he became a lawyer. After some years he was made a Member of Parliament and became one of the under-sheriffs of London.

When Henry VII died in 1509, his second son became king as Henry VIII. Thomas More was introduced to the new king in a rather strange way. He was appearing as a lawyer at the Court of Star Chamber when Henry turned up to listen. The king was not at all pleased when Thomas's brilliant speeches ensured that the Crown lost the case.

In spite of his annoyance, Henry saw that Thomas could be useful to him. Thomas rose rapidly in both the king's favour and the royal service. In 1529 he became Lord Chancellor.

But in those days it was dangerous to be one of the king's officers. There was a good deal of unrest over questions of religion. Many people protested at the way the Church was being run. They were known as 'Protestants'. Many people, including Thomas More, would have liked to see some changes made, but Thomas did not share the views of the extreme Protestants.

Then Thomas's loyalty was put to the test. The king had always wanted a son. His wife, Catherine of Aragon, had only borne him a daughter. Besides, he had fallen in love with Ann Boleyn, a lady of the Court. Henry thought he would divorce Catherine.

More and his family

The Pope was the only person who had the authority to grant divorces, and he refused to allow one to Henry VIII. Henry decided to break with Rome and make himself head of the Church of England. Then he could pass a law dissolving his marriage to Catherine.

King Henry wanted everything to seem lawful so he asked all his courtiers, officers and advisers to take an oath of loyalty to himself as head of the new Church. Most people thought it wise to take the oath, but Thomas either could not or would not.

The king went to Thomas's house in Chelsea. The two men walked in the garden and Henry did his best to persuade his friend to take the oath. But Thomas had a conscience. He had sworn to obey the Pope and could not break his promise. He offered to retire from public life.

Thomas was allowed to resign his office as Lord Chancellor. His wife, Alice, and his favourite daughter, Margaret, had done their best to make him change his mind. Alice loved her husband but she could not understand why he was being so obstinate.

Finally, the king accused Thomas of treason and had him shut up in the Tower of London. He was put on trial in Westminster Hall, found guilty and condemned to death.

Even as he mounted the scaffold, he was brave enough to make one last joke. 'Do not cut my beard,' he said to the headsman. 'It has committed no treason.'

4 Servants at Hampton Court

Who are all these people? A man named Nicholas comes forward to tell us. 'We are the servants at Hampton Court,' he says. 'Once our master was Cardinal Wolsey but he gave the palace to Henry VIII who is our new master.

'No one knows how many of us there are. The hundreds you see here all have different jobs. Would you like to know what some of them do?' We tell him that we would.

Servants at Hampton Court

Here are some of the servants we met. Nicholas says it is difficult keeping them all in order. 'Every time the king and the court are here, there may be anything up to 500 guests. We have to take on extra servants but we can't keep them once the visitors have gone.

'It's not easy to get good servants just for a week or two. Many of them are dirty or dishonest. I remember one who had to be rebuked for wiping his greasy fingers on the tapestries. Worse, I suppose, are those who take things with them when they leave. This place is so huge that the loss of something may not be noticed for months.'

Hampton Court — Clock tower

Hampton Court — Kitchens

Hampton Court — Wolsey room.

5 Loss of the Mary Rose

Everyone who likes history knows about Sir Francis Drake and the Spanish Armada but who has ever heard of the *French* Armada? Soldiers from France tried to invade England in the reign of Henry VIII, forty years before the Spanish expedition sailed.

The French Armada attacked the south coast of England to tempt the smaller English fleet out of Portsmouth harbour. At the same time, soldiers were put ashore on both the Isle of Wight and the Sussex coast.

It was an anxious time for the English. Most of their ships were driven by sails but the French had a lot of rowing galleys. Sailing ships were better when the wind was blowing but mostly the air was light and the sea smooth. This suited the galleys with their oars. They could move when sailing ships were becalmed.

Pewter jug from the *Mary Rose*

Listing the finds underwater

Arrows from the *Mary Rose*

Then, suddenly, a wind arose. The English ships set out from the harbour to fire their guns at the French. Unfortunately for Henry VIII, who was watching the whole thing from Southsea Castle, one of his vessels came to grief through sheer carelessness. This was the *Mary Rose*, a fine ship, only a little smaller than the *Great Harry*, the pride of the king's navy.

She had ninety guns on board and over 400 men. She probably hoisted too many sails too quickly and tried to make too sharp a turn. She heeled over and the sea poured in through the open gun ports. The extra weight of water made her list even more. Before the king's horrified gaze, she rolled over and sank.

Some of the lightly-clad seamen managed to swim away or were rescued from her top-masts, which were still above water, but most of the crew and all the soldiers in armour were drowned.

Eventually the French were driven off, in spite of their 200 ships and 30,000 men. There were some attempts to raise the ship but they were not successful. A few of her guns were brought up from time to time but after a while the masts collapsed, sand and mud piled up over the wreck and the very site was forgotten.

In 1965, Alexander McKee set out to find her. By then she had been at the bottom of the sea for over four hundred years. Most people said he was wasting his time; there couldn't be anything left after all those centuries, even if he could find the exact spot.

Mr. McKee wrote history books and was a keen diver. If he could only locate the wreck, what a lot it could tell us about life in Tudor times. Besides, the ship might not really be a wreck. It had only filled and sunk, not been ripped to pieces on rocks. If it was still in one piece, it was probably under the sea bed, not on it.

He managed to interest the local diving club and together they began the hunt. First of all, he had to track down every scrap of evidence that might give a clue to the ship's position. They dived for months, winter and summer, at every chance they got. They used echo sounders to try to pinpoint the site. Mrs. Margaret Rule, who had helped to excavate the Roman palace at Fishbourne, learnt to dive so that she could join in the search.

They found a low mound which they thought might be the grave of the *Mary Rose* and, after five years of searching, recovered some pieces of wood and a gun. Experts examined the cannon and declared that it really was a Tudor piece. The divers had beaten the odds and had actually found the *Mary Rose*.

In the autumn of 1982, the ship was attached to a steel frame, raised to the surface and towed back to Portsmouth. She is now in dry dock alongside Nelson's *Victory* and the things found inside her are to be displayed in a new museum nearby.

6 Rogues and Vagabonds

Imagine that you had to make a journey in late Tudor times. How would you travel? If you were poor, you wouldn't go far or very often because you would have to walk. If you were rich, you would ride a horse and take your servants with you to protect you.

There were a great many dangers. The roads were very uneven, unlit at night, and swarming with bad characters. There had always been outlaws and robbers lying in wait for travellers but there were more than ever in Tudor times. Why should this be so?

Enclosure for sheep farms was one reason. For years, landowners had been changing over from wheat growing to sheep farming, which needed fewer men. Another reason was the closing down of the monasteries. Henry VIII had ordered this to be done because he feared the monks would not accept him as head of the Church. Many lay brothers and

servants had nowhere to go. On top of that, poor people who had always relied on the monks for help now had to help themselves or starve.

There was no dole in those days. If you hadn't got a job, you had to live in any way you could. A lot of people could think of nothing better than robbing, begging, cheating and stealing. There were so many different varieties of rogues and vagabonds, we really need someone to guide us through the maze of types. Here we are, riding along a road in Tudor times and we don't know what to beware of. We see three men walking towards us. One of them looks important, so we rein in our horses and stop him.

'Oh yes, you've asked the right man,' he says. 'I'm the constable and I'm taking this wretch to the gaol in York.' We notice that one of the others has his hands roped together

behind his back. 'We could rest awhile and answer your questions. We've covered several miles already today and we'll be glad to sit down.'

He tells us of the different kinds of villain he has to deal with.

'*Thank you,*' we say. '*How do you know which is which and how do you deal with them?*'

'If a man is on the road and can't tell you why, we reckon he's up to no good. We arrest all those we can. They may be whipped, burned, branded or hanged. They can be sent back to where they came from and . . .'

'*What if they really are poor and are just looking for work?*'

'We treat them all the same. It's impossible to tell who is lying and who isn't. Just recently, we've been told to try to sort out the genuine hard-luck cases from the villains and send them to special places being built for them. However,' he says, getting up and jerking the prisoner to his feet, 'it all takes time.' He looks at us shrewdly. 'I suppose you wouldn't like to help us on our way? No, not with money, although that's very kind of you. No, I was wondering if you'd lend us your horses – just for an hour, you understand.'

We tell him we'll do anything we can and he promises to leave the horses at an inn. 'It's in the village two miles up the road,' he says, 'We'll tie them up in the stables.' He waves goodbye as they mount up and trot away.

Alas! When we get to the village, there are no horses or any sign of the men. What were they – priggers of prancers or coney catchers? No wonder they knew so much about rogues and vagabonds!

Chapter Two   The Sea and the City

1 The Spice Islands

The scene is Bristol docks in the late sixteenth century. Men are using hand winches to wind up bales, boxes and barrels from the hold of a ship. There is an extraordinary scent in the air, sweet, sharp and mysterious. If you were there, you might be able to recognize some of the different smells.

A lot of modern housewives use them when they are cooking – grated nutmeg on rice pudding, cloves in apple pies and so on.

They make the food taste nicer. We call them spices.

In earlier times, spices weren't just a pleasant extra, they helped to hide the taste of food which wasn't quite fresh. There was no tinned food then, no fridges and no deep-freezes. It was very hard to stop food going bad. If it did, you couldn't just throw it away. There was hardly enough to go round as it was.

nutmeg   ginger   cinnamon   black pepper   cloves

Christians returning from the Crusades brought back with them the first eastern spices, which was good for those who could afford the high prices. They could use spices in cooking or smother their meals with them.

Most spices were grown on some islands to the south of Asia – half-way round the world. The growers sold them to traders who took them to the coast and sold them again. They changed hands over and over again before they travelled up the Red Sea to Egypt. There was no Suez Canal then, so the cargoes went overland by camel train to the Mediterranean. Then ships took them to Venice in Italy. From there they were sold all over Europe.

The Turks captured Constantinople in 1453 and conquered Egypt. The spice routes were cut and prices rose very rapidly. Some men began wondering if there was another way to the Spice Islands that didn't mean going through Turkish lands.

A man called Christopher Columbus was convinced the world was round, at a time when most people were just as certain that it was flat. They thought a ship would fall off the edge if it went too far. Columbus said that he could sail to the Spice Islands by going round the world, sailing westward instead of to the east.

The voyage was made in 1492. After several weeks of sailing, Columbus came to some islands. He brought back gold, cotton plants and 'Indians'. Yes, he called them Indians because he thought he'd reached the East Indies. It was only after he died that people began to realize that Columbus's islands and the Spice Islands were not the same place. Even today, we have to call them the East and West Indies to tell them apart.

Columbus found America, not Asia. His theory was right; he should have been able to reach Asia by sailing west. What he could not have known was that the American continent was in his way.

The first Europeans who actually reached the Spice Islands by sailing westwards were Magellan's men. They sailed right round the world. So did Sir Francis Drake a few years later.

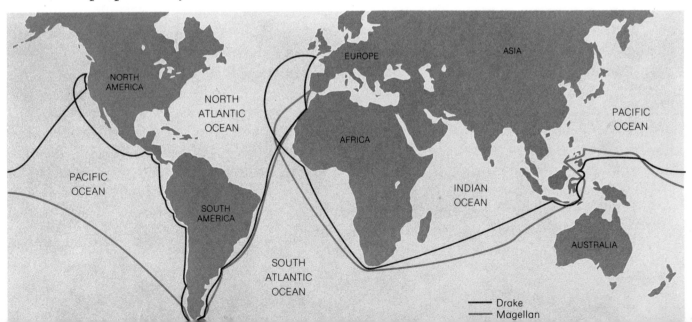

— Drake
— Magellan

2 Ship's Boy

This is a picture of Matthew Broadacre. He is eleven years old and was born on a farm in Hampshire. His father and mother worked very hard but were so poor they couldn't always feed their large family. As the children grew older, they were sent out to work on other farms.

Matthew never wanted to be a farm hand or a house servant, so just after his tenth birthday, he packed some bread and cheese in a large kerchief and set out to seek his fortune. Let's see what is happening to him.

He has always been fascinated by stories of far away places told by wandering pedlars and he wants to see some of these strange sights for himself. His footsteps lead him south to the coast. He trudges up Portsdown Hill. When he gets to the top, he sees the sea for the first time in his life.

Excited, he hurries down to the edge of Portsmouth harbour and wanders along it. A woman at an inn takes pity on him and sends out some pease pudding and a mug of ale. Her husband questions the boy and finds out that he wants to go to sea. The man knows someone on a ship in the harbour and rows Matthew out to it.

The wooden sailing ship looms huge above Matthew as they come alongside. Everything is strange and new. There seem to be several boys aboard. One of them, nicknamed Weasel, takes him to what is known as the 'slop chest' to get some clothes more suitable for a life at sea.

He is given a shirt and a short jacket. His cap is taken off his head and a loosely knitted woollen one is pulled down over his ears. His own knee-length breeches will do but he is advised not to wear the boots. He is used to going barefoot anyway.

He wonders what his duties will be. 'You might spend some of your time as a cabin boy,' says Weasel, 'but mostly you'll just be a ship's boy, like the rest of us. Come on, I'll show you round.'

They go up on deck and Weasel tells him the names of the masts and ropes and how the anchor is raised. They go below to the gun decks and Weasel explains that a boy called a 'powder monkey' has to keep fetching gunpowder and shot for the cannon when the ship is fighting.

Then they go to the crew's quarters in the fo'c's'le. It is stiflingly hot and quite dark. 'You wait till the winter,' says Weasel, 'you'll freeze in here. The only place you can have a fire in a wooden ship is on the bricks in the galley and that not often.'

They sit down to eat with the men. There is bread, cheese, dried fish and salted meat, washed down with ale. After a while at sea, the bread will run out and there will only be hard biscuit. Nearly everything else will be mouldy. Even the water will be green.

After his meal, Matthew hears the shrill notes of the bos'n's whistle calling the men to their stations. The sail setters swarm up the ratlins to the yards on the masts. Matthew goes with Weasel to help get the anchor up.

An endless loop of rope is tied in dozens of places to the anchor cable and led two or three times round the capstan. The cable is much too thick to go round it. The men sing as they turn the capstan with wooden bars and the boys have to undo the knots as they get near it, run to the bows with the lashing and make another fastening closer to the anchor.

The anchor comes up slowly, festooned with weed and smelling of slime. Men clean it and lash it to the cathead. While the sails are being set, Matthew is given a bucket and brush and told to clean the mess off the deck where the cable has dripped muddy water.

By the time it is done, the ship has cleared Southsea Castle and is beginning to roll slightly. There is an odd feeling in Matthew's stomach and he wonders, not for the last time, if he has done the right thing.

Ship's Boy

1 mainmast   2 foremast   3 mizzen   4 bonaventure   5 bowsprit
6 gallery   7 poop-deck   8 quarter-deck   9 forecastle   10 main gun
deck   11 capstan   12 helmsman using whipstaff connected to rudder
tiller   13 captain's cabin   14 main cabin—for officers and gentlemen
15 brig   16 lamp room   17 main hatch   18 galley stove   19 ships
stores i.e. sails, ropes etc.   20 ships stores food water, wine etc.
21 ballast—to help the ship's stability   22 keel   23 small deck
carronade   24 "beak"

3 Drake and Elizabeth

On board Matthew's ship is a seaman named Martin who once sailed with Drake. When he is 'watch below', Matthew loves to hear him talk about the great man.

'He is a Devon man,' says Martin proudly, 'like me. He sailed when he wasn't much older than you are, Mat, but it wasn't many years before he commanded his own ship. He made sure there was no bad feeling on board; the officers and even the soldiers had to help work the ship whenever there was need.

'From about that time, England and Spain were not at all friendly. Philip, the Catholic King of Spain, would like to remove Queen Elizabeth in order to put her Catholic cousin on the throne.'

'Who is that?' asks Matthew.

'Mary, Queen of Scots. She is a Roman Catholic but the Scots threw her out. She came to England but she is kept in prison because she keeps plotting to kill Elizabeth. A lot of people think that Philip must be behind the plots, so Elizabeth doesn't mind when men like Drake attack Spanish ships and lands.

'The Spanish ambassador used to complain that Drake was a pirate. Elizabeth pretended to scold Drake but she smiled as she did it. I think she is very fond of him and not just because he keeps coming back to England loaded down with Spanish gold. He's becoming a rich man. He has a fine suit of armour, many changes of clothes, silver dishes on his table and an orchestra to play to him when he dines aboard the *Pelican*.'

Matthew looks surprised at the name so Martin goes on. 'Yes, the *Pelican*. That was its name when I signed on. Drake changed it to the *Golden Hind* during the voyage.'

'The *Golden Hind?*' interrupts Matthew. 'Then you've actually sailed right round the world!' Martin nods. 'Tell us about it,' pleads Matthew.

'Well, we didn't know we were going round the world when we left Plymouth. Neither did the officers. The destination was kept secret. Only Drake and the queen knew that we were aiming at Peru on the far side of South America.

'There were four other ships besides the one I was on. Their names were *Elizabeth*, *Swan*, *Marygold* and *Benedict* but the *Pelican* was the only one to make it round the tip of South America and out into the Pacific. It was almost a year after we set out that we arrived at the Spanish colonies. It was a complete surprise. They weren't expecting us and we captured many ships and much gold.

'Then we sailed all the way across the Pacific to the Spice Islands, picking up a cargo of cloves there and setting sail for Africa by way of the Indian Ocean.

'We ran aground on some rocks and had to throw half of the cloves overboard. Some guns had to go too. I didn't think we'd live through it but we did. We got back to Plymouth in September 1580, almost three years after we had left.

'The Spanish were furious and wanted Elizabeth to punish "El Draque", or "The Dragon", as they called him. Our queen, bless her, would have none of it. She went aboard *Golden Hind* as she lay off Deptford in the Thames and knighted him.' Martin paused.

'As you know, Spain has decided we must be conquered. They'll be here before long, mark my words. You've joined the navy at an exciting time, Mat. You'll see as much action as you want then.'

That night Mat dreams of fighting at sea against the Spanish galleons. Before he is fourteen, these dreams will come true.

4 The Armada

In the summer of 1588, Martin's words look like coming true. Mary, Queen of Scots has been executed. Philip of Spain's only course is the invasion of England. He has collected together a fleet of about 130 ships: it might have been more but Drake sailed fire ships into Cadiz harbour the previous year. This has not only cut down the size of the Armada, as the Spaniards call it, it has also delayed the sailing.

Pope Sixtus V has blessed the Spanish ships which are to carry 30,000 men to England. Their commander is the Duke of Medina Sidonia. His plan is to sail up the Channel to the Spanish Netherlands and pick up another 20,000 men there. Then they will sail for England, destroying the English navy as they go.

Their method of doing this is out of date, according to the English admirals. Each Spanish captain aims to run alongside an enemy vessel, pull the two ships together with

Philip of Spain

grappling irons and use soldiers to capture the enemy. They have cannon but they mean to rely on small guns and muskets.

The English have given up this way of fighting. They hope that there will be fresh breezes so that they can get into the best position to fire their cannon at the Spanish without getting into danger themselves.

Matthew Broadacre is on board his ship at Plymouth. He is nearly fourteen now and has become a powder monkey. The admirals of the fleet are also at Plymouth. They are Lord Howard, Hawkins and Drake. They are waiting for the Armada to appear.

A small ship puts into port. The crew have sighted the Spaniards heading eastward. Beacon fires are lit on hilltops to tell our soldiers to stand by. Elizabeth goes to Tilbury to encourage her troops.

Drake doesn't want to get in front of the Spaniards – he prefers to pick them off from behind – so he must wait until they have passed Plymouth. He calmly goes on with his game of bowls.

Matthew makes sure everything is ready at the guns he will serve. Soon the order is given to put to sea. The weather is unsettled. It is not hot and calm as it was when the French tried the same thing over forty years before. The English seamen don't mind. They know that the weather favours them. They believe that they are better sailors than the Spaniards, or 'Dons', as they call them.

For a week they follow the Armada along the Channel. Sometimes the English captains sail their ships nearer to the huge galleons and fire at them. Then all is excitement on Matthew's ship. He hurries to and fro with the gunpowder while the gunners ram the shot home with long poles.

A glowing slow-match is put to the touch hole. There is a blinding flash and an ear-splitting explosion. The gun bucks, and swirls of gassy smoke billow across the deck. Other guns do the same.

One or two Spanish galleons are damaged

The Armada

but most of them come safely to anchor at the place where the troops are to be embarked. Drake decides to send in fire ships, just as he did at Cadiz.

Eight old vessels are filled with tar barrels, brushwood and gunpowder. They are drifted towards the Spaniards during the night. Their crews leave it to the last minute before lighting the fires and then escaping in the rowing boats.

The Spaniards panic. Anchor cables are cut before the crews are on deck. The galleons drift about and collide. Some run on to sandbanks. Drake's men keep up the bom-bardment. Matthew has run so much he can scarcely keep to his feet.

To add to the confusion, a southerly gale begins to blow and the galleons have to run before the wind, many of them badly damaged. Drake's ships follow them right up the east coast until they run out of shot and powder.

The proud Armada is scattered far and wide. Most find themselves alone the next day. Their only hope is to get back home safely. They have to sail right round the British Isles. Strong winds wreck more of them on the Scottish and Irish coasts.

In all, Philip has lost nearly eighty ships and over 10,000 men. He goes on trying to beat England but for Elizabeth and her people, the danger is over, thanks to Drake and the English seamen — not to mention the boys who also served.

5 London Life

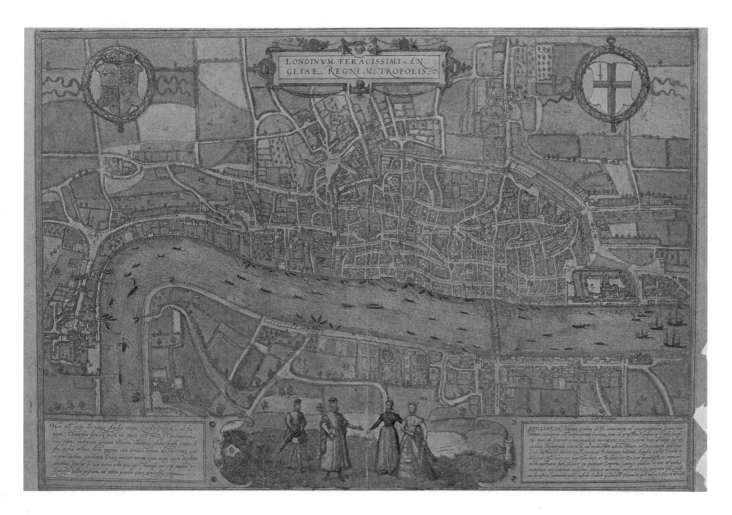

Even in the sixteenth and early seventeenth centuries, London was fast becoming one of the great cities of the world. It had about sixty or seventy thousand people when Henry VII came to the throne in 1485. At Elizabeth's death in 1603, the numbers were three times as great. Cities were such unhealthy places in which to live that the new generation of babies hardly replaced the numbers who died. Most of these extra citizens had come to London from all parts of England.

The area of the old Roman city had been about half a square mile. Much repaired, the walls and gates still stood but there were houses and other buildings spilling out beyond, into the open countryside.

Many newcomers to London had to take lodgings if they wished to live inside the walls. If they wanted a new house built, it would probably have to be alongside one of the roads leading away from the capital or in Southwark, to the south of the River Thames. Here were the theatres, the bear-baiting and cockfighting pits. These were not allowed inside the city which was run by the guilds and merchants.

The streets were narrow and no cleaner than they had been in the Middle Ages. Houses were still mostly of wood, and in London were often three or four storeys high.

Let's walk along the streets of Tudor London as if we are tourists. We've come down from Colchester on the main road through the villages of Stratford, Bow and Mile End. We go through Aldgate (the Old Gate) and notice the pump at which people are queuing for water. Very few buildings have water laid on.

London Life

Straight ahead is the road leading to the Royal Exchange. This is where merchants meet to do business. It was built by Sir Thomas Gresham in 1571.

Just beyond is St. Paul's Cathedral. This picture doesn't look like the one we know. It is the old church, dating from the Middle Ages. Surrounding it are the booksellers' and printers' shops. All sorts of people have stalls set up here and along Cheapside. Almost anything you want can be bought from the stalls but there are also a great many pedlars, with their goods in barrows, on their backs or in boxes or trays slung round their necks on leather straps.

Everywhere there are churches and inns. The streets are full of people and animals. There are no dustmen or street cleaners. All sorts of rubbish and filth lie about on the rough dirt roads or clog up the cobblestones.

Of course, there aren't any empty tins or plastic bags; the rubbish is straw, bits and pieces of vegetables, shells of eggs or oysters and even bits of rotten meat.

Some rubbish is dumped in piles at the

Tower of London

London Bridge

end of the road. These attract rats and mice. Every now and then, the filthy conditions lead to outbreaks of the plague.

We'll head towards the river where the air may be fresher. All the way along the Thames, there are steps, landing stages and wharves. Here are landed all the things needed to keep London going.

All is bustle and excitement as men busy themselves with loads of corn, vegetables, fish and coal. Vessels are tied up the entire length of the north bank and the river is swarming with small craft.

In the distance we can see the grey outline of William the Conqueror's Tower. That is easy to recognize but what are the three odd-looking buildings on the south bank? One of them has a flag flying over its thatched roof. A mass of people seems to be making its way to the Globe, as the building is called. We could hire a boat to take us over but it's easier to go with the crowd and cross the Thames by the only bridge.

London Bridge stands on nineteen brick pillars and the space between any pair of them is only big enough for a rowing boat. As the tide turns, the river water pours through the gaps and forms waterfalls. You can hear the dull roar of the water as you walk between the houses that line the bridge.

The Globe

6 The Globe

When we get nearer, we can see that the Globe is a theatre. We would find the place very strange. The Tudors would be equally puzzled by the way most of us see plays. We sit in our own homes and turn a switch on the television. We settle back to watch. We don't often think of how the pictures get on the screen.

In the television studio cables snake across the floor, cameras move about silently, microphone booms hover over the set and batteries of powerful lights shine down. The pictures and sounds are turned into electrical pulses and broadcast. Miles away, the aerial on our roof picks up the signal and our TV set changes it back into voices and faces.

The actors in the studio aren't doing anything very different from what actors have done for centuries. Just before Tudor times they had started giving plays in the open courtyards of inns.

When special theatres were built, the designers used the inn yard as a pattern.

A television production of *The Tempest*

There was a flat, open space with a wooden platform sticking out into it. The bedroom verandas of the inn became the balconies of the playhouse.

The balconies surround the stage on three sides and a seat in one of them costs a shilling. A stool at ground level is sixpence. It is only tuppence to stand in front of the stage.

Most of the seats are taken, so we stand with the 'groundlings' and wait for the play to start. A trumpet sounds and the audience is still. There are no curtains and very little scenery. As there aren't any lights either, the performance always has to take place in daylight.

A man comes from a door at the back to announce the setting. The play is *The Tempest*. A few ropes are draped about to show that the first scene is on board a ship. Some of the cast are making noises off stage which are supposed to sound like a storm at sea.

It is not thought decent for women to appear in plays. Boys take the female parts. If they stay with the company, they will be able to play the men's roles when they grow up. At the end of each scene the actors all go off together.

Sellers of sweets and drinks wander round looking for customers. There may even be a pickpocket or cutpurse at work in the audience. They are often lucky because the playwatchers sometimes get so interested that they forget to guard their money.

By the time *The Tempest* has come to its end, the sun is beginning to set. The audience drifts out of the Globe and soon the theatre is empty.

The Globe

Chapter Three   Years of Unrest

1 The Gunpowder Plot

Bonfire night! The frost in the air makes the flames seem even brighter. Rockets hiss upwards, bangers explode and sparklers make little pools of light. The children and their parents eat baked potatoes as they watch the guy burn.

Why do we call it a 'guy' and why do we burn one every fifth of November? To get an answer, we need to go back to the year 1606.

It is a bitter January day. A large crowd stands in front of the Parliament buildings. Some men are about to be hanged. We ask one of the spectators who the criminals are.

'The Gunpowder plotters,' he answers. 'They tried to blow up Parliament and now they are being punished.'

'How did they do that?'

'I'd better tell you the whole story,' says the man. 'When Elizabeth died, the King of Scotland was her nearest living relative, so he became James I of England – and also head of the Church of England.

'There are three main groups of Christians in the country now as there were before James became king. There are those who still look to the Pope as their head, the Roman Catholics, that is. The Anglicans accept the king as their head but they have made the religion simpler. The third group think that they have not made it simple enough. They don't want bishops, candles, robes, ceremonies or anything like that. They want the Church purified, they say, so we call them Puritans.

'When it seemed that James was not very sympathetic to the Catholics, a small, desperate gang of them decided to murder him and the whole of the government. A man called Catesby gathered the gang together and one of them, Thomas Winter, went over to Flanders to persuade a young soldier named Guido Fawkes to join them.

'Guido, or Guy, was born in York in 1570. He was brought up in the Church of England faith but his father died and his mother married again. Guy's stepfather was a Catholic so Guy changed his religion. He went to Flanders and became a soldier in the Spanish army.

'The plot was explained to Guy. Thomas Percy, another of the gang, had rented a house next to the Houses of Parliament. They were going to tunnel through into the basement of Parliament, and stack barrels of gunpowder in it. When the king, Lords and Commons met, they would blow the whole lot up.

'There was to be a rising of Catholics in the countryside. The plotters would take over the government and choose their own ruler.

The plotters in the cellar

'As it happened, they were able to hire a cellar under the House of Lords and the idea of tunnelling was dropped. They stored over one and a half tons of gunpowder there in thirty-six barrels and waited for Parliament to meet.

'Unknown to them, one of their number sent a warning to Lord Monteagle. The cellars were searched and Guy Fawkes was caught red-handed. He had a dark lantern and a fuse which he was going to light the next day – fifth of November, it would have been.

'He was taken to the Tower and tortured to make him give away the names of his fellow plotters but he wouldn't. Some of the others tried to start the revolution anyway but it came to nothing. Most were either killed or captured.

'The eight that were caught were put on trial. All were found guilty and sentenced to death. They were dragged here behind horses from the Tower this morning. Aren't you going to stay and see them hanged?' The man sounds surprised.

We murmur an excuse and push our way out of the crowd. We've seen all we need.

Now we know why the figure we burn is a 'guy'. As to bonfires, people have always lit them when they are glad. They were very pleased the explosion hadn't taken place.

Unfortunately for the masses of ordinary Catholics, feeling remained strong against them for over two hundred years. Some of them went overseas to start a new life in America where they could worship as they pleased. Strangely enough, so did many of the Puritans.

2 Witchcraft

King James I seemed to be a rather obstinate man who liked to have his own way. He thought he knew more than most people about a number of subjects. He even wrote a book called *Daemonologie*, in which he set out what he and most people believed about witches.

The word 'witch' nowadays most likely makes you think of an old woman in black, riding a broomstick and wearing a tall, pointed hat. Like elves and magic, witches are interesting to read about but nobody really believes they exist. Once upon a time, it wasn't only the children but their parents too, who believed in them.

For three hundred years, from about 1400 onwards, so-called witches were hunted down and killed in most Christian countries. Things

were not quite so bad for suspected witches in England as they were in Europe, but they were bad enough.

In those days, it wasn't so easy to get a living. There were no experts to tell you why your wheat had the blight, why your hens weren't laying or why your cows had stopped giving milk. Being human, you would look for someone or something to blame.

'What about that old woman who lives alone at the end of the lane? They say she's a widow but she's lived by herself for so long that no one in the village can remember her husband. Her only friend is a cat and she's often seen about the village muttering to herself as she gathers plants from the hedge-rows. What does she do with them?' Probably no more than make simple medicines but you are ready to believe that they are wanted to make a magic brew.

It's whispered that she'll cast a spell on

someone for you if you ask her. Perhaps that was all there was to be said but people were much more ready to believe in magic than they are now. It took no more than a slight neighbours' quarrel to make her a suspect.

As soon as you told your friends that you thought the old crone had put a spell on your farm and its animals, there were sure to be some who would remember similar tales, each trying to tell a more dramatic story than the last.

Back in the Middle Ages, it used to be the Church's job to try the witch cases. Since Tudor times, it had been the ordinary courts that had to deal with witchcraft. When James became king, he made death the punishment for all kinds of witchcraft.

The victims were nearly always women, and elderly ones at that. Many of them didn't even know what was happening to them. Others seemed to enjoy the excitement of being the centre of attention and freely confessed to all the charges.

We don't now think that these poor old women had any special powers but people then lived in a world where magic was accepted. As far as we know, the only way a witch could harm you was to tell you that she had cast a spell on you. If you were so frightened and ignorant that you believed her, then some damage might be done.

Unfortunately, superstition was very strong and many witches were hanged. In Europe, witch hunts were officially organized and many thousands were executed. In England it was usually left to ordinary people to report their suspicions; there was only one occasion when officials went out looking for witches.

Matthew Hopkins and John Stearne travelled through eastern England for three years, beginning in 1644. An accusation was enough to prove guilt in their eyes. A confession tidied up the whole thing, so the two

'witchfinders' threw their victims into ponds to see if Satan would help them to float. If this didn't bring a confession, the suspects might be kept without sleep for days and nights on end.

Hundreds of arrests were made and dozens of witches were hanged. In fact, Hopkins got so good at 'sniffing out' witches, that people began to suspect that he was one himself. Finally, he was tried as a sorcerer and hanged in 1647. Witch trials went on for another seventy years after his death but the numbers of executions grew smaller until in 1736, the witchcraft laws were at last done away with.

3 The Colonies in the New World

In a churchyard at Gravesend on the Thames there is a memorial to a Red Indian princess who died in 1617 and was buried there. What was a Red Indian doing in England at that early date? To find out, we'll have to look at the beginnings of America.

You have already read about some English people going to the New World so that they would be free to worship God in their own way. It wasn't just religious men and women who went, however. Many were attracted across the Atlantic Ocean by the promise of riches.

The end of the war with Spain came in 1604 and it seemed to Englishmen that this was their chance to go and look for gold in North America as the Spaniards had done in South America.

In May 1607, three ships landed in Virginia with over a hundred colonists. Some were meant to set up a village of wooden huts, to clear trees and to plant food crops, while the rest went off to look for gold and silver.

The trouble was that everyone wanted to search for gold and none wanted to stay and work. Disease and starvation followed and many died. John Smith took charge of the colony but they had to rely on the local Indians for food. After a while, the Indians became less friendly and they took Smith prisoner.

The Indian chief, Powhaton, ordered him to be killed but his daughter, Pocahontas, pleaded with her father for the Englishman's life. The chief was merciful and Smith went back to Jamestown, as the settlers called their

village. Pocahontas went with him. Eventually she married one of the colonists, a man named John Rolfe. He took her to England but our climate was fatal to her and she died here. She was only twenty-two.

In the meantime, the Virginia Company in London decided to send out more colonists. Six hundred men, women and children were packed into eight ships which set sail for America. One of them, the *Sea Venture*, ran aground in Bermuda. Shakespeare read about the wreck and used some of the detail in his play *The Tempest*.

The rest reached Jamestown but were no more ready to work hard for the colony than the earlier party had been. Again, disease and starvation carried off many of them. Some even took to cannibalism!

More people arrived from Britain and in less than thirty years from the first landing, there were over 5,000 white settlers. Strangely enough, the thing which really saved Jamestown was the tobacco plant.

The Colonies in the New World

Raleigh was the first man to bring tobacco to England. He and other explorers had noticed how the Indians dried the leaves, rolled them up, set fire to one end and sucked smoke from the other. In Europe the habit spread. The leaves were chopped up and smoked in a pipe. The first pipes had a nutshell for a bowl with a straw for a stem, but before long, pipes were being made of baked clay. More and more tobacco was grown in Virginia and sold in England. Jamestown and Virginia went on to prosper.

Other European nations set up their own colonies in the New World; there was also another English colony. This was started by a hundred Puritans who sailed from Plymouth in the *Mayflower*. They were driven off their course by winter gales and landed far to the north of where they should have been.

In December 1620, they gave thanks to God for their arrival and for the freedom to worship Him as they wished. Their new land was on Cape Cod and they named their little village Plymouth.

Unlike the Virginian settlers, the Pilgrim Fathers, as we know them, were sober and hard-working. They built log cabins, cleared a nearby stream for a water supply and planted corn. Seeds and cuttings were set in the little gardens round the cabins but few survived: the first winter was very hard. Without the help of the Indians, they would have starved.

Indians showed them how to get by during the worst of the blizzards. They brought maize seeds to the colony and taught the Puritans about the local plants and animals. Slowly, the settlement grew. More colonists came to make a new life in 'New England'. In only a few years the settlement was doing more than just survive – it had become prosperous by means of trade and sheer hard work.

4 Civil War in England

James I died in 1625 and not many people mourned him. He had ruled for years without asking Parliament's advice and his son, Charles I, showed signs of doing exactly the same thing. English people feared that he would marry a Catholic princess and they didn't like the idea of a new line of Catholic kings.

Eventually, Charles married Henrietta Maria, the sister of the French king. England then blundered into a war with Spain but when Charles asked Parliament for money to pay for it, the members refused. Charles tried to carry on without them or the money.

The war went badly, so the king once more had to ask Parliament for funds. Again they refused. Charles tried every way he could think of to raise money. Even forcing people to lend it to him, or compelling them to feed his troops was not enough. Those who refused were put in prison without trial.

Parliament said that if the king would stop doing these things they would give him what he wanted. He agreed but the money was not well spent and the king was forced to make peace with Spain.

Not all the quarrels were about money. Parliament wanted a bigger say in the running of the country but Charles, like his father, believed in what he called 'the divine right of kings'. This, he explained, meant that as God had made him king, no one had any right to question anything he did.

Another disagreement was over religion. The members passed a resolution against the Catholic faith. The king sent them home and ruled without them for eleven years – but he still needed money as badly as ever. Most of the ways he had of getting it angered different groups of men. He charged landowners taxes on estates that had been in their families for generations. He demanded 'ship money' not only from those who lived on the coast but also from those whose homes were miles from the sea. Anyone who disagreed or refused was punished.

Then Charles tried to interfere with Scotland's religion, but the Scots would have none of it. They raised an army and invaded the north of England. Charles couldn't pay his own soldiers, many of whom didn't want to fight the Scots anyway. Parliament was called yet again. Before the king could ask the next Parliament for tax money, they passed a law saying that the king couldn't dismiss them if they didn't want to go.

Charles was very angry. He went with a band of 300 soldiers to arrest some of the more troublesome members but they had been warned and were not in the House of Commons.

Most of the members left Westminster for the City of London where they felt safer. The merchants and Puritans started to get ready for the struggle they felt sure would come. Some of the powerful landowners began to arm their tenants for the king's protection. The two groups began to refer to each other by insulting names. The king's men called the Parliamentary side 'Roundheads' from the short-cropped hair many of them wore. The Royalists were known as 'Cavaliers' which means 'swaggerers' as well as 'horsemen'.

The street mobs in London rioted and became so violent that Charles thought it wiser to leave the capital. He went north to York where he set about raising an army. He was not to see London again until the war was over.

5 A Royalist Family

What did the king's friends think of what had happened and what did they do about it? Perhaps we could ask one of them. We'll have to travel to the north-west of England because that is where his home is.

Sir Henry Moxon seems pleased to see us. He and his wife Ellen take us inside their large manor house set in acres of parkland. We are led into a richly furnished room. A servant brings wine and we sit down on comfortable leather chairs.

While we are waiting for the rest of the family, we look about us. There is a fine stone fireplace with glowing logs propped up on andirons. The walls are covered with oak panelling and the ceiling is beautifully moulded with leaf and flower shapes. There are two or three oil paintings hanging on the walls in gold frames.

The late afternoon sun slants in through the lattice windows and the light falls in hazy patches on to the rich Turkey carpets. The furniture is solid and heavy.

A Royalist Family

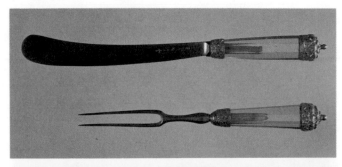

Jacobean cutlery

The light begins to fade as we sip our wine. Lady Moxon tells a servant to light the candles. The maid brings in a tinder box and strikes sparks with a flint and steel. She catches a spark in the tinder, a scrap of scorched cloth, and blows it into a flame. She thrusts a wooden spill into the flame. When it is alight, she closes the tinder box and lights the candles with her match, as it is called.

The candles are set in silver sconces fixed to the wooden panelling. The flames waver as the door opens. It is Sir Henry's son, Richard, his wife, Mary, and their three young children.

We are surprised to learn that there are two boys and a girl, for two are dressed as girls and only one as a boy. He is twelve and his name is Andrew. His brother is only three and it is the custom for young boys to wear girls' clothing until they are about six or seven. The two older children are dressed in the same way as the adults. Elizabeth, the girl, is nine.

We talk with the family while the servants lay the table for the evening meal. We can see from the fine, stylish clothes everyone wears that they must be very well off. We are sure of this when we glance at the table. Nearly everything on it is of silver.

The adults sit at the table and the children have bowls and spoons and a chair each by the fire. The meal is mostly meat dishes such as pork, lamb, venison, duck, pigeon and so on. The sauces are served in separate dishes and there is more wine. We end with almond and honey cakes, sugared fruits and cornflour pudding with jam.

'Well,' says Sir Henry, 'I believe you want to know why we are for the king? The reasons are quite simple. In fact, they all come down to only one reason and that is because he is the king. If a man takes up arms against his lawful sovereign, that is treason. There is only one way to deal with traitors.'

'That is true,' says Richard, Sir Henry's son, 'but my father has left out all the other reasons. We don't want a lot of low churchmen telling us how to lead our everyday lives. More important, we don't mean to let them interfere with our religion.

'My father and I have only a week left before we join the king's army. One of my cousins who lives nearby will move in here to look after our families. Another cousin . . .'

'Don't talk about him,' growls Sir Henry. 'He is no longer a kinsman. My brother's son feels that His Majesty is wrong to oppose the will of the people and has gone off to London to fight for the Parliamentary army. God will punish him for his wickedness.'

Soon after this, we take our leave. We don't tell Sir Henry but we are going to visit the armies of both sides shortly.

6 Royalist and Parliamentary Soldiers

The Roundhead, or Parliamentary soldier, nearly always fought on foot at the start of the war. He could be a pikeman or a musketeer. He wears a metal helmet with a flexible neck cover and face protectors. A leather coat and gauntlets to match, plus a high, plain collar go on the top half of his body. Some soldiers have a back and breast plate as well. The foot soldier wears knee breeches and woollen stockings but the horse soldier has long leather riding boots which hide the stockings. It is rather surprising to find that the boots can be worn on either leg. There was no shaping to the feet of shoes and boots in those days.

The cavalryman has a leather sword belt slung across his chest from the right shoulder. The sword sheath then sits on his left hip and the weapon is easier to draw out.

You will notice that complete body-armour seems to be less common now. Both sides have guns but most of the fighting is still hand-to-hand, so some protection is needed for the head and chest.

Cannon in the Civil War have not advanced much since Elizabeth's day.

Hand guns are complicated and not very accurate. The musketeer wears a bandolier over his shoulder. It is a belt from which hang little containers of gunpowder.

The musket is so heavy, it is hard to fire from the shoulder. The musketeer has to support the far end on a forked stick. Loading the gun takes time. First, the soldier has to stand the gun on its wooden stock. Then he empties the gunpowder from one of the containers into the muzzle and rams it down with a rod. The bullet is a round lead ball which is also rammed down. A piece of wadding is tapped into place to stop the ball rolling out and the powder spilling.

As the musket comes up to the firing position, some of the powder trickles into the pan at the side. The soldier pulls the trigger and a flint snaps down on to a grooved steel plate, rather like the action of the tinder box. Sparks shoot into the pan and light the gunpowder. The line of grains leads down to where the main charge is, behind the bullet. The explosion drives the ball out of the muzzle.

It takes several minutes to go through the drill. Clumsy as this weapon may sound, it is better than the old matchlock gun which many of the soldiers still have to use.

Prince Rupert is the commander of the Cavalier horsemen. He was only twenty-three when the war started but he is a daring and experienced soldier. To begin with, the Royalist cavalrymen did not dress very differently from the way they did when they went hunting. Apart from the pieces of armour that some of them wore, you could tell who they were from their bright, coloured clothes, the lace at their throats and wrists (and even over their boot tops!) and their plumed hats.

The cavalry played an important part on both sides. It was some time before the Parliamentary units were as large or as good as the king's.

Prince Rupert and his brother, Prince Maurice, were usually too good for the Roundheads to beat. They often drove large sections of Roundhead troops off the battlefield, only to find that the battle was over by the time they got back, and not always won for the king.

On 22 August 1642, Charles I set up his headquarters at Nottingham. The king's party was stronger in the north and west and in the countryside rather than the towns. The south and east, the seaports, and particularly London, were for Parliament. The king decided to strike at London and end the war quickly.

7 The Battle of Edgehill

At Nottingham Charles called on his loyal subjects to join him. When he first raised his standard, he had only 300 foot soldiers and not quite three times as many horsemen.

The recruits flocked in. As soon as he was ready, Charles moved westward to collect more men from the Welsh border area. Against him was the Earl of Essex, commander of Parliament's army. Let us ask one of his Roundhead troopers what happened to stop the king getting to London.

'My name is Peter Pike. I suppose with a name like mine I should have been a pikeman but My Lord Essex made me a musketeer when he found I could shoot.

'The king moved off to Wales to pick up his extra men. We were meant to stop his army but they got past us somehow and we didn't pick them up until they were on the way back from Shrewsbury to London.

'We followed so hard upon their heels that part of our rearguard got separated. We couldn't slow down, for the king's army had a good two days' start of us. We reached Kineton and could hardly believe our luck. The Royalists were camped only seven miles away. It was 22 October 1642.

'By now, there were as many Cavaliers as there were of us but they were all together in battle formation whereas some of our men were still miles to the rear.

'The king sat on his horse in his golden armour, surrounded by his own bodyguard. Between him and us were the lines of Royalists. On the king's right was Prince Rupert and most of their cavalry. In the centre were the foot soldiers, with a smaller group of horsemen on his left. More important, the army was at the top of a steep slope known as Edgehill.

'I suppose the Royalists thought we might surround them and starve them out. At all events, they left their hilltop and came down to our level.

'Rupert and the horsemen of the left charged before the rest of the army was formed up. We weren't ready for him and our left flank got pushed back. Luckily, one of our regiments that had arrived late met them in Kineton. John Hampden's foot soldiers they were, as I remember.

'Rupert struggled back to the battlefield with what was left of his squadrons and found that the king's infantry had taken a bit of a mauling – not surprising really, when you think that they had no horsemen to protect them.

Charles's headquarters in Oxford

'While Rupert and his men were away, the king's cannon were captured and so was his standard, at least for a while. Oliver Cromwell's regiment did well in the battle but when the Royalist horsemen came back, things were even again.

'After a while, both sides broke off the fight and took stock. No one had won and many men had been killed on both sides, perhaps as many as 5,000 of them.

'Lord Essex decided that the battle at Edgehill would have to be left as a draw and he ordered us to form up and march back south-eastward, so we could block the road to London. Charles took his army to Oxford, and set up his headquarters there for the rest of the war.

'There was talk of peace but Rupert struck at our army just before we got to London. There was a skirmish at Brentford Bridge and the king's cavalry stormed the town on 12 November. Then the Trainbands, or part-time soldiers, came out from London in strength. They formed up at Turnham Green and the Royalists retired to Oxford. It's the nearest they are going to get to the capital.'

Edgehill today

The Battle of Edgehill

The map shows the position of the two sides
at the beginning of the battle.

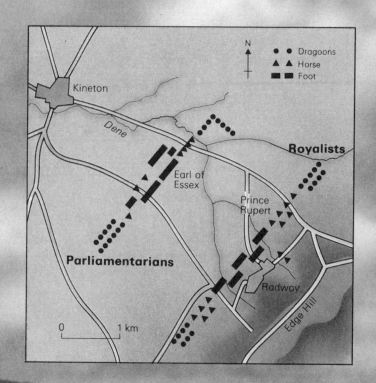

N

● ● Dragoons
▲ ▲ Horse
■ ■ Foot

Kineton

Dene

Royalists

Earl of
Essex

Prince
Rupert

Radway

Edge Hill

Parliamentarians

0   1 km

8 Oliver Cromwell

What sort of a man was Cromwell? It's rather difficult to answer this question. For one thing, Cromwell was not a simple kind of man and for another, we know very little about his early life.

We know that he was born at Huntingdon in 1599, towards the end of Elizabeth I's reign. We think his father was a farmer but he might have been a brewer as well. Oliver attended the local grammar school where he was taught by a Doctor Beard. The good doctor drummed into him that God watches everyone and punishes wickedness. It was probably from Doctor Beard that Oliver got his first strict Puritan ideas, although his enemies were later to say that he wasted his time at school wrestling and playing cricket.

At the age of seventeen, he went to Cambridge to study law but his father died a year later and he went back to Huntingdon to farm the family estate. He married his wife Elizabeth when he was twenty. He must have had to work hard for he now had to support his wife, his mother and five sisters.

He still had time to help his neighbours when they got into trouble with the authorities so it isn't surprising to find him becoming a Member of Parliament for Huntingdon in 1628. There he spoke for the persecuted Puritans.

No one really knows where he learned how to command soldiers – perhaps it just came to him naturally.

If there was one person who learned a lesson at Edgehill, it was Oliver Cromwell. He saw the importance of well-trained cavalry. Back in East Anglia, he began to recruit and drill his Ironsides, as they were called.

Oliver Cromwell

They were mostly farmers and nearly all were Puritans. They took their religion seriously and, unlike most soldiers, agreed that they would not swear, gamble, ransack captured towns or get drunk. Cromwell worked them hard until they could fight or fire on command and break off a chase when ordered, something which Rupert's gallants never learned to do.

Cromwell demanded that only proper professional soldiers should lead the Parliamentary troops. Sir Thomas Fairfax was appointed Commander-in-chief and Cromwell was made Master of the Horse.

Training the New Model Army

Cromwell reorganized the troops so well, they were known as the New Model Army. It was to be a strong, well-disciplined body of men, dressed in uniforms and paid regularly at the rate of two shillings a day.

On 14 June 1645 came the last main battle. This was at Naseby near Leicester and the pattern was the familiar one of Rupert's cavalry dashing off after some of the Roundheads and leaving their foot soldiers without cover. Cromwell's own horsemen made short work of the Royalist infantry and Charles I had to be held back. He wanted to gamble his last few reserves and himself in the battle. His advisers persuaded him not to.

He rode north to Scotland, hoping the Scots would remember that his father was Scottish too. The Scots took him and sold him to the Roundheads but the army and Parliament couldn't agree as to what to do next. Cromwell was a member of both the army and Parliament and he tried to sort out the quarrels that arose over what form of government and religion there should be in England.

Charles, now in Carisbrooke Castle on the the Isle of Wight, tried to stir up the disagreements. He lost any trust either side might

have had in him. He managed to get the Scots to invade England once more – this time as Cromwell's enemies.

Cromwell had to fight and win all over again. He was bitterly angry at what the king had tried to do. Those Members of Parliament who wanted to bargain with Charles were turned out of the House of Commons and Cromwell found himself in charge. Now neither king nor Parliament was ruling England. The army was in control and Cromwell was its leader.

Oliver Cromwell's hat

9 The Trial and Execution of Charles I

This is Westminster Hall. If you visit it when there are not too many visitors about you may be able to sense the ghosts of the past. It was the chief law court of England for over 600 years. Here Thomas More was tried for treason in 1535. Here, too, Guy Fawkes faced his accusers seventy years later. Both were found guilty.

In 1648, Cromwell's army was firmly in control of the country. The king was brought from prison in Hurst Castle and lodged at Windsor while workmen fitted out this very hall for the unusual trial it was to see.

Many members of Parliament no longer went to the House of Commons as they disapproved of what Cromwell was doing. The remaining Members appointed 135 commissioners as judges but only about seventy of them agreed to take part. The problem was that no one knew how the trial was to be run. Many argued that such a trial was itself unlawful for the king was to be accused of treason. How could a king be a traitor? Surely the word 'traitor' means one who is disloyal to his king?

But Bradshaw, the president of the court, Cromwell and a few others were determined to go ahead and nothing could stop them. Afraid of attacks by the king's supporters, Bradshaw wore a steel-lined hat throughout the trial.

A plate in the floor of Westminster Hall marks the spot where the king sat. The chair he used had been specially made for the occasion.

Bradshaw read out the charge of high treason and asked the king if he pleaded guilty or not. Charles replied that, as the court had no authority to try him for any crime at all, there was no point in his saying anything.

Witnesses told the court how Charles had made war on his own people. Charles repeated that the judges had no authority to try him and that he alone had the right to speak for his subjects. He insisted, 'A king cannot be tried by any superior jurisdiction on earth. If power without law can make laws, I do not know what subject there is in England that can be sure of his life or anything he calls his own.'

It didn't make any difference. Cromwell and Ireton, his son-in-law, had decided the king must die. Thomas Fairfax, who had been one of Cromwell's loyal supporters, withdrew from the trial. Lady Fairfax shouted from the gallery that it was Cromwell, not the king, who ought to be on trial.

However, fifty-nine of the judges signed the death warrant. Many protested later that Cromwell and the army had forced them to do it. On 27 January 1649 Charles was brought in to hear the sentence of the court. This time he tried to deny the charges but it was too late.

Three days later he was taken from St. James's Palace to Whitehall. At one o'clock in the afternoon, they led him out through a window of the banqueting house on to a wooden scaffold outside.

Thousands of people were waiting for him. Hundreds of soldiers were drawn up several ranks deep around the platform in case there was an attempt to rescue him. They had even provided ropes to tie him down if he struggled. Charles smiled calmly and scornfully at these. He said that he would die a good Christian, that he forgave his murderers and that he was dying for the good of the people. Then he arranged to signal the headsman when he was ready.

He knelt, laid his head on the block, said 'Remember,' and gave the signal. There was a groan from the crowd as the axe came down and a louder one when his head was held up for all to see.

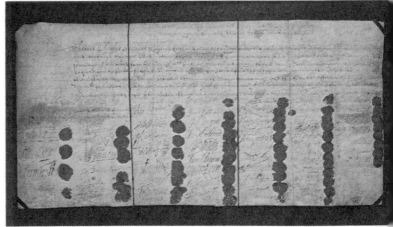

Charles I's death warrant

10 The Commonwealth

Even when the war was over, there were still three main Christian religions in England – the Catholics, the Anglicans and the Puritans. The freedom which the Civil War had brought encouraged all sorts of new ideas – some of them rather strange – in both government and religion.

For example, the Levellers wanted England to be a republic with complete freedom of worship. The Diggers thought they had a right to take land anywhere and farm it for themselves. They started to plough and sow seed on common and waste land but they didn't last very long.

Many of these odd sects thought that they alone had found the way to God and that everyone else was wrong. If you were not an

Anglican or a Catholic, there were many different groups to which you could belong.

They included Independents, Presbyterians, Baptists, Calvinists, Muggletonians, Fifth Monarchy Men, Seekers, Manifestarians, Family of Love, Ranters, Arians, Adamites and Libertins.

Most did not last more than a few years, although some thrived and are still in existence to this day. Among the surviving groups are the Quakers. In the next section, we will meet a Quaker family but before we do, we ought to see what had been happening after Charles I was beheaded.

Very often, the feeling of bitterness which leads to a civil war goes on for years after it is over. The execution of the king made that

The Lord Protector

feeling deeper and more lasting. Ireland and Scotland had immediately hailed his son as Charles II. Some of the colonists in America felt the same way.

Cromwell smashed the Royalists in Ireland and then turned to Scotland. Charles II, as we must now call him, promised to make allies both of the Catholics and the Scottish Presbyterians in his struggle against Cromwell.

Cromwell beat one Scottish army at Dunbar and defeated another at Worcester in 1651. Charles was forced to hide in an oak tree in order to give Cromwell's men the slip. He eventually escaped and managed to get back to France.

Within two years, England was called the 'Commonwealth' and Cromwell himself had become 'Lord Protector'. Some even wanted to make him king.

However hated Cromwell was by some people, it is true to say that he gave England a period of peace and made its name respected throughout Europe.

Charles hiding in the oak

11 A Quaker Family

This is a house built in the new style. Large timber beams for building have been getting scarcer. Houses from now on will mostly have to be made of bricks or stone, at least for the outside walls. Here, in a busy town not far from the capital, Isaac Penton, a well-to-do carpenter has moved with his family.

His wife is called Beth. His three sons are Josiah, Elias and Samuel. Among Quaker families, biblical names are often given to the boys. The girls are called by words which, until this time, were only used to describe someone's character. The two grown-up daughters are Prudence and Charity and the twelve-year-old girl is known as Patience. This is also a common practice in Quaker homes.

Isaac is a master craftsman. He makes cabinets, chests and furniture. He even does woodcarving, if his customers wish. He employs men to help him. Josiah works for his father but Elias, who is eleven, and Samuel, aged nine, are still at school.

The first thing you will notice from the picture is that the clothes are very dull. Gone are the bright colours and fancy lace-work of the Cavaliers. Most Puritans prefer not to show off with gaudy garments and long, curly hair but the Quakers nearly always dress in black or grey with touches of white here and there.

The Quaker movement was started by George Fox. He had become convinced that many people went to church on Sunday only because they had to and that they recited the set prayers like parrots, without really understanding them. He believed that each person could find his or her own way to God without the guidance of bishops or even priests and that this could be done through Christ's help, given to those who kept up a struggle against the temptations of a wicked world. Quakers thought deeply about their religion, prayed in their own words and read almost nothing but the Bible.

Fox travelled the country preaching the new life to all who would listen. He made many converts, among whom were the Pentons. They lead their lives according to the words and actions of Jesus, as shown in the New Testament.

The Pentons, like all Quakers, believe that there should be no ranks or classes in society and that all people are alike, as God's children. Once upon a time in England, a man might use the words 'you', 'your' or 'yours' when the person he was talking to was an equal or a superior, and 'thee', 'thou' or 'thine' when addressing an animal, child or servant. The Quakers use 'thee' and 'thou' to everyone to show what they think of this system. In the same way, the Pentons talk to each other and to strangers in the words of the Bible.

A Quaker Family

It is morning in the kitchen of the house. The walls are white, the doors of plain wood. There is a lattice window. A dresser with crockery stands against the wall. A long wooden table is laid for breakfast. There are earthenware dishes and mugs on it.

Beth serves out the boiled oatmeal porridge but before they eat, they all kneel on the stone floor to say grace. Everyone in the family takes a turn at thanking God and the others say 'Amen'.

After breakfast, the two youngest boys go to school. Josiah makes his way to the workshop at the back of the house whilst Isaac sits down to write out a bill for one of his customers.

Beth and the girls get on with the usual

George Fox, founder of the Quakers

household tasks. Unlike the housewives of our own time, she has to make many of the things we are content to buy from shops. As well as jam, preserves, butter and cheese, she also makes candles and even the ink her husband is using.

There is little time for play among Quaker children. Quakers don't approve of wasting time and they don't like amusements such as singing and dancing. If the girls sing at all as they work, it is a psalm or a hymn. Life is very serious in a Quaker family.

12 Crime and Punishment

We've already seen how strict the different kinds of Puritans were. Cromwell's Ironsides didn't drink, swear, gamble or brawl and the Pentons thought singing, dancing and the display of fine clothes were wicked. Soon, many of these ideas were put in the form of laws.

To see that they were carried out, Cromwell divided the country into eleven districts and did away with the old system of judges and juries. Over each district he set a major-general with a number of soldiers to carry out his orders.

Most people did not like this military rule, not only on account of its strictness but also because it interfered in the way people lived. Cromwell's government made the mistake of trying to force people to be good.

Cromwell's Parliament made new laws against bull- and bear-baiting, play acting, cockfighting, travelling or trading on a Sunday, and so on.

We can understand why cruel sports involving animals should be banned but it wasn't the cruelty the Puritans objected to, so much as the gambling and drinking which went with them. Besides, Parliament distrusted any gathering of more than a few people because they might be plotting against their rulers. This was perhaps why play-going was outlawed. Not only were there many citizens in the same place, they might also be corrupted by an anti-Puritan play.

Horse racing, playing cards or dice for money, even football and wrestling were forbidden. It seemed to those with no strong views on amusements that the Government was out to spoil their fun.

They could picture someone in a London office examining these and other pastimes one by one and asking, 'Do people enjoy this? If it pleases someone, it must be wicked and ought to be stopped!'

Local soldiers were often ordered to burst into private houses to see if any of these 'moral' laws was being broken and whether those inside were living their lives according to the Good Book.

There was no mention of May Day frolics in the Bible, so the troopers chopped down the maypoles. Nowhere in the New Testament did it say you should celebrate Christ's birthday by eating a lot of food. There were cases of troops seizing Christmas dinners as they were

Title page of a book attacking amusements

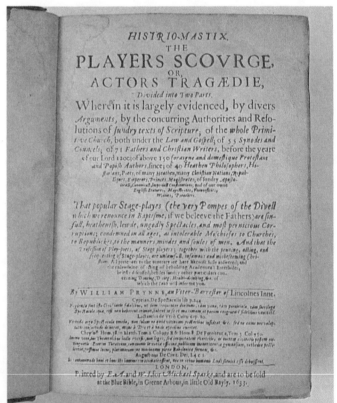

HISTRIO-MASTIX.
THE
PLAYERS SCOVRGE,
OR,
ACTORS TRAGÆDIE,
Divided into Two Parts.

By WILLIAM PRYNNE, *an Vtter-Barrefter of Lincolnes Inne.*

LONDON,

Printed by E. A. and W. J. for Michael Sparke, and are to be sold at the Blue Bible, in Greene Arbour, in little Old Bayly. 1633.

cooking and taking them away.

The main punishments for crimes such as theft, assault, robbery or murder, as well as the breaking of the new 'kill-joy' laws, included fines, imprisonment, the stocks or pillory and hanging. In those days many different offences could result in a hanging and at least one of the other punishments could also end in death.

For example, the Puritans believed that a public shaming hurt the offender as much as anything else. A village drunk might be put in the stocks or made to wear a wooden collar with a large 'D' (for 'drunk') painted on it.

Passers-by might jeer at a man in the stocks or sling mud at him but if they were really angry at what he had done, they could throw stones.

A man in the stocks could dodge some of them but the pillory didn't allow much movement. Sometimes the authorities nailed the criminal's ears to the wood to make sure.

Other sentences were slitting the nose, cutting off the ears and branding. It's strange to think of the love of God being used as an excuse to carry out these horrible punishments.

Stocks at Woodstock

13 The Countryside

We need someone to guide us through the counties of England in Stuart times. By good fortune, we are able to get Mark Rudge the pedlar to show us around. He is going to let us travel in his cart, so that we can see for ourselves what England was like just over three centuries ago.

'I'm sorry it's not very comfortable,' he says as he helps us up. 'The roads are very bad – all bangs and bumps in the summer.'

'Why just the summer?'

'Because the roads are mostly bare dirt. In winter, the sun doesn't dry up rainwater and the roads are seas of mud. Few people use them in the winter. Those who do, leave ruts in the ooze which are likely to bake hard when the weather gets warmer again. That's what makes the jolts; the wheels slip down into the ruts and pot holes.'

'What about springs on the axles?' we ask, but Mark doesn't know what we are talking about. 'We are lucky we aren't right behind another cart,' he says, 'or we would hardly be able to breathe for the dust.' He flicks his whip at the horses and we trundle on.

He shows us the hop-fields and orchards of Kent. It is blossom time and the trees are covered in pink and white flowers. We travel from village to village selling the things that the peasants can't grow or make for themselves. They are mostly luxuries such as fancy buttons, lace, combs, hair ribbons, toys and so on.

Mark says that the hop-field and orchard villages of Kent and Worcestershire are good places for him to trade because the farmers sell nearly all they grow and live on the money they get. Villages near large towns

grow wheat, barley, rye and oats and raise animals on a large scale. They too sell most of their produce and thus have money to spare.

'The villages that don't have a lot of coins to spend,' says Mark, 'are those that are too far away from the markets. They go in for what we call champion farming. I think it comes from a French word. It means they have huge fields and they don't really grow things to sell — only to eat. When we've been through London, I'll show you a village like that.'

A few days later, he is as good as his word. 'Here we are,' he says. 'Jump down and I'll tell you about it.' We wander round the tiny hamlet looking at the little cottages.

'The people here grow their own food and not much else. In a normal year they get by, in a bad one they go short but in a good one they may have a little left over to sell. That's where people like me come in. There are quite a lot of travelling salesmen.

'The tinker mends pots and pans. Then there are the sellers of hoes, sickles, scythes and spades. Some go about with barrels of tar, salted fish or salt on its own — anything, in fact, that the villagers can't get locally.

'They have a few long, narrow strips of land in each of the three big fields you can see. One field grows wheat, one barley and one lies fallow to allow time to get goodness back into the soil. The animals are turned into the fields to eat the stalks when the harvest is in.

'There's a meadow for hay: they cut that and store it to feed a few animals through the winter. Otherwise the cows and sheep graze on the common and the pigs root about in the woods.

'They are peasants and they live like peasants. It's lucky that I'm with you. A few years ago they'd have stoned you out of the village just because you're strangers. "Foreigners", they would have called you. They don't do that now but they aren't too friendly with folks they don't know.'

We are glad when Mark's business is done and we can leave.

Chapter Four   The Restoration

1 Charles II

At first, the Puritans were admired by many people, particularly during the reigns of those rulers who had persecuted them. Unfortunately, the Commonwealth gave the Puritans the chance to show that in some ways they were just as narrow-minded and intolerant as their persecutors. They tried hard to force everyone into the mould they approved of.

There were disagreements between those who had won the Civil War: arguments between the different religions and quarrels between army and Parliament. After a few years many people had grown weary of Cromwell's rule, but there was little they could do about it. At least he kept the arguers in their place and prevented any one group from getting on top.

Cromwell's death mask

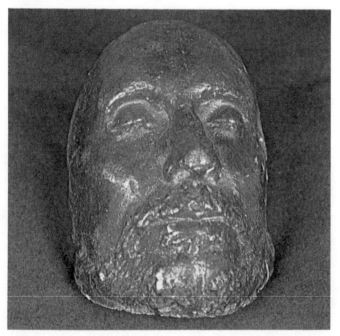

Just when it seemed that England might be getting back towards a better system of parliamentary rule, Cromwell died. One of the things he did before his death was to name his son, Richard, as the next Protector.

'Tumbledown Dick', as people began to call him, was not the man his father had been. He preferred to run his own estates in the peace and quiet of the countryside.

As soon as the different quarrelling groups realized that there was no one in control of England they began to make plans to take over. It looked as though there might be

Charles II on his way to London from Dover

another civil war. It was then that General Monck took charge. He was a soldier who had fought for the Cavaliers at the start of the war but who had changed sides.

He commanded the Commonwealth army in Scotland and was trusted by most people. He marched his men to London and declared that there must be an election.

The new Parliament came to an agreement with Charles II. Many of the laws passed in Cromwell's time were to be cancelled. Charles said he would not seek revenge on those who had fought against his father. On one point his advisers were firm: the men who had actually signed the death warrant must be brought to trial.

With these things settled, Charles II set out to cross the Channel. General Monck waited at Dover. On 25 May 1660, Charles landed and made his way slowly up to London amid cheering crowds. They were only too glad to have someone who might be able to keep order and save the country from war.

The Ironside soldiers who had fought so fiercely against Charles I now stood to attention on Blackheath and saluted his son as he passed by. Then the new Parliament paid them off and sent them home. England had had enough of large peace-time armies.

When it came to punishing the killers of the late king, a difficulty arose. Fifty-nine men had signed and sealed the document condemning Charles I to death. About twenty of them had fled abroad, a similar number were already dead, leaving only about eighteen to stand trial.

To Charles II's credit, he did his best to see that as few men were executed as possible. In fact, only nine of those who had signed were put to death. To many Royalists, this seemed to be too small a number. Still thirsting for vengeance, some of them dug up the bodies of Cromwell, Bradshaw and Ireton and hanged them.

2 Charles's Court

In 1698 a fire burned down almost all of the old palace at Whitehall. The only part left was the Banqueting Hall from which Charles I had walked to his death. In spite of this, Whitehall before the fire had been one of Charles II's favourite palaces.

There were several other palaces at which Charles II could have held his court. There was St. James's which had been used by Henry VIII but Charles II didn't like it and it was not a royal dwelling again until the reign of his niece, Mary II. Hampton Court and Windsor saw the Royal party from time to time but the court was almost always to be found at Whitehall.

The palace covered twenty-three acres. If it had been a regular shape it might have measured 100 yards by 1,000 yards. In this maze of buildings there were about 2,000 rooms and many hundreds of servants.

We'll see if they will let us in. There are two main entrances. The first is on the river. You could hire a boat and land at Whitehall steps but we'll go the other way, down a narrow lane with a guarded gate at each end. Today we are lucky and the sentry passes us along. We have to go through another gate flanked by guards but soon we are in the Outer Chamber.

Here are all the rest of the men and women who have come to see the king. Sometimes the nearest the visitors get is the gallery of the Banqueting Hall. Every day at noon, Charles II dines in public. For many visitors, to catch a glimpse of the king eating was enough.

Some of those in the Outer Chamber are dealt with by minor secretaries. Those that are

Charles' Court

left are taken through into the king's Presence Chamber. Most of them are seen by senior advisers.

The king has a lot of these – the Lord Chamberlain, the Lord Steward, the Master of the Horse, the Earl Marshall and so on. We are not lucky enough to be shown into the Privy Chamber but after a moment, the king comes out of his office. He claps the man nearest to us on the back and laughs loudly. 'Well, Sir Peter,' he says, 'we shall give this matter some thought and let you know anon.'

We notice his striking appearance. He is tall with masses of dark hair, a small black moustache and a friendly smile. We don't have time to see much more. The king bows to two very beautiful ladies in fine clothes and has gone. The audience is over before it had properly begun. The courtiers get ready to leave.

On the way out, we fall into step with Sir Peter who guides us to the gate. We pass the queen's apartments, the tilting ground, the cockpit and the tennis court. 'His Majesty feels that his people went too long without pastimes under Cromwell,' says Sir Peter. 'He himself likes the things which the Puritans

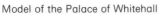
Model of the Palace of Whitehall

stopped. Now the king and all his subjects can gamble, go horse racing, watch a play or even sing and dance if they feel like it.'

'*The king is fond of dancing, then?*'

'Indeed. He likes the ladies – and why not? Why should he not have beautiful people about him at court?'

'*What exactly is a court?*' we ask.

'It consists of the king and queen, their advisers, servants, friends and acquaintances. There are those who wait on the king because they want a favour from him – a grant of land, the right to trade, a title, perhaps, or something of that kind.'

We say goodbye to Sir Peter when we reach the exit. We wonder what sort of reign Charles II will have. His main occupation seems to be having fun but his eyes are those of an intelligent man. He won't be able to do as he likes with Parliament, though; the time when a king's lightest word was law has gone for ever.

The Banqueting Hall today

Key to Whitehall Palace: **1** King's private apartments **2** gate **3** tennis court **4** cockpit **5** banqueting house **6** formal gardens **7** horse guard yard **8** chapel **9** great chamber **10** kitchens **11** bakery **12** sawpit **13** coalyard **14** woodyard **15** privy stairs **16** bowling green **17** guard house **18** palace gate **19** River Thames **20** palace wharf

3 A Poor Family in London

These archaeologists are digging on the south bank of the Thames, almost opposite the Tower of London. They are looking for remains of the seventeenth century, not for traces of Stone Age men or Romans. One of them holds up a bowl. It is blue and white and known as 'Lambeth Delft'. Modern archaeologists are not the only people to have found Lambeth bowls at this site. There is one in the room shown opposite.

This room is in a London house at the start of Charles II's reign. The family which lives here are lucky that their room is at ground level. The house has four floors and many rooms, all occupied by different families. It lies in a narrow street near London Bridge.

Like the other buildings in this street, it is quite old and mostly made of wood. The inner walls are plastered to about waist height and lime washed above. The ceiling is very low. There is little furniture, as you can see. A bed, a couple of chests and a table are all roughly made of wood. There are three or four stools but only one chair.

Finds from the seventeenth century

An open fireplace will burn wood if the family can afford it. Coal is more plentiful but it doesn't burn as well without an iron fire basket. When there is a fire, mother can boil water and do simple cooking but if she wants to give her family puddings or pies, she must buy them from the cook-shop on the corner. She gets her bread from the baker's down the lane.

Apart from the iron pot on the fire, there are not too many cooking utensils. A good deal of the time the family eats cold meals in a cold room. Hot meals may consist of porridge for breakfast and soup with bread the rest of the time. Meat is very rare in this family.

There are wooden platters, rough earthenware bowls and wooden spoons on the table for the mid-day soup. On the chest under the window stands the blue and white bowl.

Now we'll meet the family. There are five members: the parents and three children.

A Poor Family in London

There is a baby, not much over twelve months old, a girl called Sarah, aged eight, and a boy of nine named Jem. Let's hear from the mother how the family manages.

'I look after the family as well as I can. I do all the usual chores such as cooking, cleaning and sewing. I also do some needle-work for the neighbours.

'Father works long hours in a new brick-field a few miles to the east of the city near a village called Stratford-at-Bow. He wheels loads of roasted bricks from the ovens to the stacks and has to walk to and from his work. His wages are tenpence a day and the cost of living is rising. It's hard to make ends meet but he's lucky to have a job at all.

'Neither Jem nor Sarah go to school. Lessons cost money and there isn't enough to spare. I try to teach the older two to read. Sarah knows her ABC but Jem is bored with books and is happier roaming the streets.

'It's just as well I'm handy with my needle, for clothes are expensive too. I buy second-hand garments, cut them up and remake them. I can't make hats or shoes though. Sometimes we are given "throw-outs" from richer houses. Otherwise we have to go without. Father is the only one who must have shoes. Fancy shoemakers are out of the question but even a pair from the cobbler's takes almost a week's wages. Hats are even more expensive. We don't wear these drab greys and blacks for religious reasons — we have no choice.'

Sarah and Jem help their mother about the room. Jem's task is to fetch water for the day from a nearby pump for cooking and drinking. There is no tap in the house. No one

in the family takes a bath, nor do they wash very often. Their thick clothes never get cleaned.

Jem can go out when he has brought the water. He may earn a copper or two running errands or holding gentlemen's horses. He also has a happy knack of finding things. It was he who found the Lambeth Delft bowl. If we go with him this morning, he will show us where he first saw it.

4 The State of the City

As we leave the house we glance back and are surprised to find that it isn't the familiar half-timbered type that we already know. The bottom part of the wall is made of stones and pebbles stuck together with stiff clay. Above it the whole side of the house is covered with overlapping boards, like a boat. Everything is tarred.

Our second surprise is the state of the roads. In some places there are cobblestones or patches of gravel. In others, someone has paved a stretch with flat stones. The rest is just hard-packed dirt. There are no pavements. It has been raining and there are puddles everywhere.

Jem doesn't seem to mind and splashes straight through them, his bare legs getting even dirtier. We pick our way across the drier patches. It would be difficult to do this at night, as there are no lamp posts to be seen.

One or two buildings have lanterns on brackets which are fastened to the walls but they only have candles and wouldn't give much light. It's a good thing Jem is leading the way, or we would quickly get lost. There are no sign posts, street names or house numbers.

There is rubbish everywhere, including a huge pile at the end of Jem's street. It doesn't smell very pleasant but the boy doesn't seem to notice. Above the stench of decay we can detect other scents every now and then – a wave of stale, drink-laden air from the ale-house, the pleasant aroma of baking bread and a general drift of salt, tar and spices from the direction of the River Thames.

Jem has agreed to show us round the city before we go to the place where he found the bowl. We follow him past the fish market at Billingsgate and hold our noses. We turn away from the busy, bustling docks and wharves, where all kinds of cargoes are being unloaded. We can still see the tops of the wooden cranes above some low warehouses as we climb a steepish street towards the end of London Bridge.

This is still the only way of crossing the river on foot, although Jem says you could hire any one of over 2,000 rowing boats to take you over. We come to the main road and plunge into the mass of people thronging it. This street is in better condition and there are lines of wooden posts at the sides. These are to stop the waggons and coaches crashing into the buildings.

If you wanted to feel safe, you could walk between the post line and the houses. You wouldn't get run over but you might get a bucket emptied over your head from an upstairs window. In any case, the ground nearest the houses is very muddy. None of the roofs has a gutter or drainpipe, so the rainwater just runs down the tiles and pours over the edge.

We glance curiously as a fashionable lady passes in a sedan chair. Street hawkers and traders all shout their wares at once. London is a noisy, dirty city.

Jem takes us to see the city wall and some of its gates. The wall is broken or crumbling in places. Elsewhere, the only thing holding it up is a shop or house built right up against it. The moat which once surrounded the capital has long been filled up with rubbish and built over.

At last we cross the bridge to a factory on the south bank. Alongside it is a long, low mound on which the workmen throw the pots and plates which are not good enough to be sold. Jem can't find an unbroken pot or bowl but suddenly he straightens up with a coin in his hand.

Hardly has he stood upright when another urchin snatches it from him and runs off. He is

The Common Cryer

126

soon lost to sight. When we suggest telling the police, it is Jem's turn to look surprised. 'Police?' he says. 'What is that?'

5 The Plague

It is 1965. Mark, who is eight, has come to school early to show his teacher a curious object which he is carrying in a plastic bag. Some children in the playground are singing, 'A ring, a ring of roses, a pocket full of posies, atishoo, atishoo, we all fall down.'

'Hallo, Mark,' says Miss Fellows. 'What have you got there?' Mark shows her the object. 'My brother found it sticking out of the dirt in a front garden when he was on his paper round,' he says. Miss Fellows knows what it is and phones the police. A week later they go to the station to meet the police surgeon.

'You were right, Miss Fellows,' says the doctor. 'It's part of a human skull. We've done some tests and asked some questions and this is what we've found out.

'It was probably a man aged about twenty-five to thirty-five but he wasn't murdered. He died about three hundred years ago, possibly of disease. We think the house where your brother found it was built on top of an old plague pit.'

They thank him, collect the skull and later, put it in the school museum. Mark wants to know about the plague.

'Could you catch it from the skull, Miss?'

'No, Mark. It was passed from person to person by the fleas which lived on rats. We don't really know where the plague started – the Far East, perhaps. We think it was brought here by rats on ships. The piles of rubbish attracted the rats and they also built their nests in houses. People weren't very clean then and every summer hundreds died of Bubonic, as we call it now.

'In the summer of 1665, London and many other parts of Britain had their worst attack since the Black Death, over three hundred years before. This time hundreds of thousands died. No one knew what caused it nor how to cure it. Doctors thought that the bad smells might be responsible for the plague. They wore strange head-dresses stuffed with sweet-smelling herbs hoping they would be

Plague cottage at Eyam

Plague victims' graves at Eyam

protected. Some of their remedies were even stranger.

'As soon as a case was known, the house was closed and nailed up for forty days. The people inside could starve to death even if they weren't infected, unless they had friends who could supply them with food. There wasn't a street without at least a few houses boarded up and with a red cross painted on the door. Sometimes you could see where someone had scrawled underneath the cross, "Lord have mercy on us".

'So many people passed away that the bodies piled up faster than they could be dealt with. Carts rumbled through the streets at night, the driver shouting, "Bring out your dead." The corpses were buried in dozens or even hundreds in huge holes. This is where we think your skull came from, Mark.

'Some people tried to escape to the countryside but took the disease with them. The tailor at a village called Eyam in Derbyshire had some clothes sent to him from London. He died a week later. Within a month over twenty more people had died also. The village parson took a terrible decision. He talked the villagers into cutting themselves off from the rest of the world in case they spread the plague.

'Friends left food at the parish boundaries

and washed the money they got for it in vinegar baths. It was late in 1666 before the villagers were free of their year of terror and by then there were only about ninety of them left. Before 1665, there had been 350.'

Mark is very interested and goes to close the window to shut out the song the children are singing. 'Don't, Mark,' says Miss Fellows. 'Listen to the words. Rings of roses were the red spots on your body which told you that you'd got the plague. The posies were the flowers they thought would keep the disease away. Atishoo stands for the sneeze that was the plague's first sign. That little rhyme has lasted 300 years.

'And what,' Miss Fellows ends, 'what, Mark, do you think "We all fall down" means?'

6 The Great Fire of London

As well as the plague and the dirt, one of the drawbacks of living in a town in those days was the danger of fire. Most of the houses were made of wood and many of the roofs were thatched with reeds.

At that time, there was not much you could do if your house caught fire. If it was a small fire, you might be able to douse the flames with buckets of water, provided that there was a stream or pump nearby. When the thatch caught fire, the householder might try to pull down the bundles of smoking reeds with a long hook and stamp out the sparks.

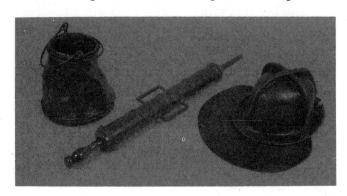

A few families owned syringes like this one, but they didn't hold very much water. More often than not, fires were just left to die out of their own accord. On 2 September 1666, a fire started in London which could not be put out and which refused to die down for nearly a week.

The day before was a Saturday. That night, a baker named Thomas Fariner had stoked up his oven so that he could get a good start the next morning. He was woken up even earlier than he had planned.

In the small hours of Sunday morning, he and his wife coughed in their sleep and woke up to find the bedroom full of smoke. Quickly throwing on what clothes they could find, they shook their servant girl from her sleep. Escape seemed out of the question, as the staircase was already well alight.

Thomas and Mrs. Fariner made their way up to the attic, scrambled through the dormer window and slithered across the thatch to the next house and safety. The servant girl was too frightened to follow them and they never saw her alive again.

The baker's house was in Pudding Lane near London Bridge. The neighbours were alarmed but no one else was – there were always fires in London. However, there had been a hot summer and everything was as dry as tinder. To make matters worse, there was a stiff breeze blowing.

The flames reached the thatch and the wind carried wisps of burning reed to an inn standing on Fish Street Hill. Stores of hay and straw blazed up and the wind blew the sparks about. Within an hour or two, the whole street was ablaze and the fire was heading towards the warehouses by the Thames.

The Lord Mayor of London was woken by servants. So was Samuel Pepys, Secretary to the Navy, who later wrote in his diary for that day that although the fire was a large one, it was not near enough to cause alarm. Pepys went back to sleep again but the next day he went to have a closer look.

He hired a ferryman to row him along the Thames. By the afternoon of 2 September, dozens of houses had been destroyed, along with inns, stables, warehouses and even a church or two. Pepys asked the boatman to take him to Westminster. He reported to the king who told him to give orders to blow up

houses in the path of the fire. Pepys went back to tell the Lord Mayor. That night he watched what was happening from an inn on the far bank of the river.

Before it grew light the next morning, Pepys was alarmed to find the flames sweeping towards his own house. He took his best wine, all the documents from the Navy Office where he worked and a large cheese and buried them in the garden.

By 8 September the fire had been halted. Much of London lay in smoking ruins. The streets could hardly be seen under their piles of half-burnt timber and heaps of ash. Those who had fled at the height of the fire carrying their valuables now crept back in ones and twos to gaze sadly at the destruction. More than 10,000 houses and over eighty churches had gone, including St. Paul's, whose roof had rained molten drops of lead.

The strange thing was that only six people had died in a fire which had destroyed more than half of London. There wasn't a lot to be cheerful about but one good thing was that the fire seemed to have burned out the plague, for it never returned on the same scale again.

The last page of Pepys's diary

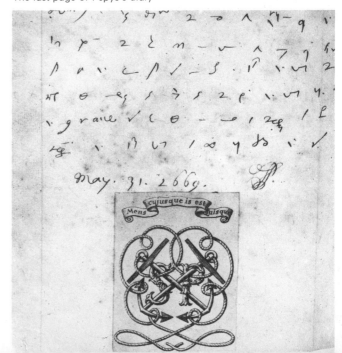

The Great Fire of London

7 Wren and St. Paul's

Nearly sixty years after the Great Fire an old man died, aged ninety. He was Sir Christopher Wren. Born before the Civil War when Charles I was still alive, he lived to see the end of the Stuart line. He died in the reign of George I.

In the days following the fire, his much younger figure was to be seen picking his way carefully through the smouldering heaps, pacing, measuring and taking notes.

Within a week he was able to show Charles II his plans for rebuilding the city. The design showed wide avenues of fine stone and brick buildings leading to a new St. Paul's as the centre of the capital.

Unfortunately, few of his grand ideas were realized. The rubbish from the fire took weeks to remove but as the streets were cleared, the owners of the land started to rebuild their houses and shops. Of course it would have been nice to get rid of all the narrow courts and winding alleys, but to broaden or straighten a road meant taking somebody's land away from them. Finally, most of the plan was dropped. Some tidying up of building lines was done but it was more like patching a torn garment than making a new one.

Something would have to be done about the places of worship, however. More than three-quarters of the city's 109 churches had gone. It was decided that there had been too many churches. In future there were only to be fifty-one and Wren was put in charge of designing all of them. After the first few, Wren found himself so overworked, he merely outlined his plans for the others in a general way and then left the details to his assistants.

St. Paul's Cathedral today

As Surveyor-General to Charles II, Wren had to make sure the new building laws were obeyed. These said that at least the main roads must be widened and that all new shops, houses and so on must be made of brick or stone if they were inside the city walls.

In six years, London was rebuilt, the money for the public buildings coming from a tax on coal. One building remained as a huge ruin from the Great Fire. St. Paul's Cathedral was beyond repair and would have to come down. This wasn't an easy task, for there were no power machines to help the workmen. Almost 50,000 cartloads of rubble had to be taken away.

Wren drew up his plans for a St. Paul's completely different from the old church. The work began in 1673 but details of the design were changed from time to time as the walls rose.

He lived in a little terraced house on the south bank of the Thames while the work was going on and perhaps wondered sometimes if he would ever live to see it finished. In the meantime, Wren went on with his designs for other buildings. Oddly enough, he had begun as a professor of astronomy at Oxford. He was not really an architect at all but he had started drawing up plans for buildings even before the Great Fire.

He was sixty-five before even part of the cathedral was finished. This was the eastern end and it was opened to the public in 1697, when William III ruled England.

Another thirteen years were to pass before the work was completed. At the age of seventy-eight, Wren had himself pulled up on ropes and winches to the top of the building, a height of more than 350 feet, so that he could see the last stone laid. The year was 1710, during the reign of Queen Anne.

He died in 1723, aged ninety. He had lived long enough to see England governed by no less than eight different rulers. He was buried in his own cathedral. A simple stone marks the place. It says: 'If you are searching for his monument – look around you'.

8 Art in Stuart Times

The making of beautiful things is one of the aims of art but during the Puritan Commonwealth, art was not encouraged. After Charles II's restoration, it is not surprising to find that English artists were in short supply. Portraits were popular in the late seventeenth century but the painters were mostly foreigners. Milton was the most important writer of the time.

Painting of Charles II by Van Dyck

Frontispiece of Poems by Milton

Wood carving by Grinling Gibbons

Painting of Nell Gwyn from the Studio of P. Leley

Painting of Samuel Pepys by T. Hays

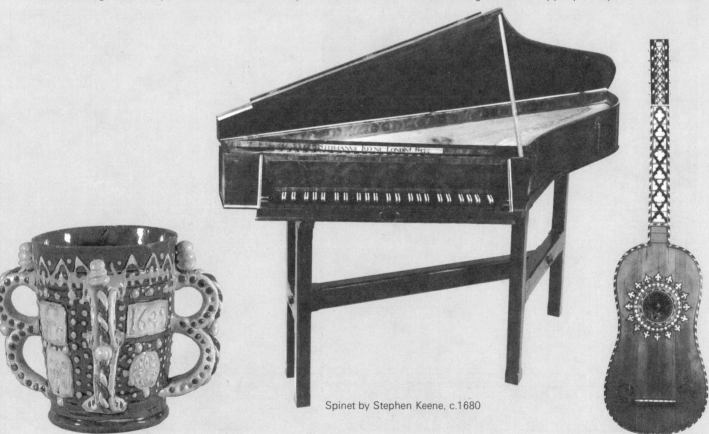

Lead-glazed four-handled cup

Spinet by Stephen Keene, c.1680

Guitar attributed to Jean Voboam, c.1680

9 Architecture in Stuart Times

If there was no outstanding painting in the Stuart period, there was certainly a great deal of good architecture. The rebuilding of the London churches destroyed in the fire was in the hands of Wren and Hawksmoor but Vanbrugh and Winstanley were designing magnificent country houses for the great landowners.

Sir Christopher Wren by G. Kneller.

Quebec House, Kent

Rufford Old Hall, Lancashire

St. Mary-le-Bow, 1671–80

Interior of St. Mary-le-Bow

St. Andrew's, Holborn Circus, 1686

Sudbury House, Derbyshire

Blickling Hall, Norfolk

Audley End, Essex

Castle Howard, North Yorkshire

99

Chapter Five   The Last Stuarts

1 James II and the Monmouth Rebellion

Charles II died in 1685 and, although he had several children, none of them could claim the throne, for none were the children of his own wife. One of them, the Duke of Monmouth, was quite sure his mother had been married to Charles and he did not see why he should not be the next ruler.

He had been the king's favourite son and did not take kindly to the idea that his uncle James should be the king. However, Parliament thought otherwise and Charles II's brother ascended the throne as James II. There was nothing Monmouth could do; he was out of favour and living abroad in Holland when his uncle became king.

James II

His friends argued with him that, as James II was a Catholic, a lot of people would support a Protestant like himself and would help him gain the throne — by force if need be. Help was promised in fitting out ships and finally the duke agreed to a rebellion against his uncle.

Three ships were to sail to Scotland to stir the Scots up against James, whilst the Duke of Monmouth would head for the west of England where there was supposed to be a better chance of getting recruits.

The Duke of Monmouth landed at Lyme Regis in June 1685. Straightaway he sent men about the town to tell everyone that James was not the rightful king and that they should fight for the duke.

Monmouth was handsome, popular and, most important, not a Catholic. Men came to join him by the hundred. Soon he had about 6,000 followers.

They may have been keen but they were not really an army. A few had been soldiers but most knew nothing of fighting and had few proper weapons. Worse still, the leaders couldn't always rely on the men to do exactly what they were told. All the same, there were enough of them to frighten the townsfolk of Axminster and Taunton, which they captured.

The news alarmed both James II and his Parliament. The duke was declared a traitor and an outlaw. A reward of £5,000 was offered for him, dead or alive. James collected what troops he could and ordered them down to the west country.

A playing card of the time

Unluckily for Monmouth, he didn't realize that there were several deep ditches between his men and the king's camp. One of his rebels stumbled into a ditch and his gun went off. This was enough to alarm the regular soldiers and the ditches stopped the two armies grappling with each other straightaway.

In the end there could only be one result. The king's soldiers stood their ground and shot down Monmouth's peasants by the hundred. When the battle was over, the duke's dreams were ended. Nearly all the Sedgemoor rebels were taken prisoner. A few, including the duke himself, tried to escape. He was captured near Ringwood in the New Forest and executed on 15 July 1685. His rebellion had lasted about five weeks all told.

The king's army caught up with the rebels on Sedgemoor. By this time, Monmouth had heard that the Scottish part of his plan had failed, so he made up his mind to launch a surprise attack at night.

The rest of the prisoners were tried by the hard-hearted Judge Jeffreys. Something like two hundred of them joined their leader on the scaffold. More than eight hundred were shipped to Barbados in the West Indies and sold into slavery.

To this day, surnames in Barbados can be traced back two hundred years to the west of England and 'Monmouth's Rebellion'.

Duke of Monmouth pleading for his life

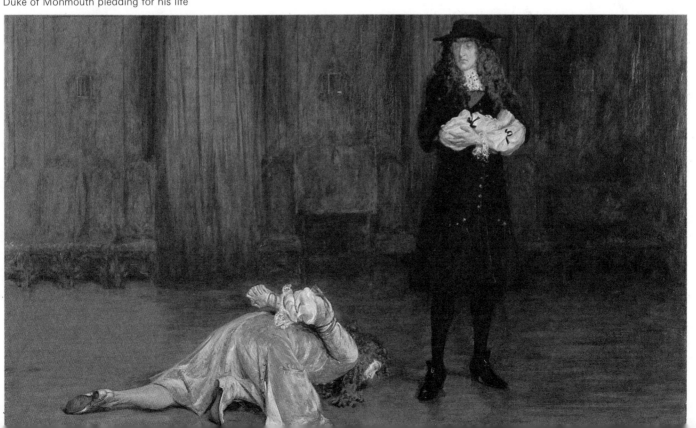

2 The Glorious Revolution

James II managed to survive one attempt to force him off the throne but he wasn't so lucky the second time. He was not a clever man but he was a stubborn one. Once he got an idea in his head nothing would shift it.

He became a Catholic late in life and looked for ways to change the religion of England. His first wife had been a Protestant and James's two grown-up daughters, Mary and Anne, were the same.

By now, England was a thoroughly Protestant country and wanted nothing to do with the Pope in Rome. This didn't stop James. Even though he knew there were laws to stop Catholics being officers in the army or navy, he appointed several of them to senior positions.

He increased the size of the army and went to inspect the soldiers at their camp on Hounslow Heath. Parliament was alarmed at the things he was doing, and protested strongly. James decided to copy his father, Charles I, and rule without a Parliament.

His elder daughter, Mary, was already married to a Dutch Protestant prince named William of Orange. A few important people slipped quietly over to Holland to ask his advice about what James II was doing. What should they do? Surely William and Mary as Protestants were also alarmed at the way James was trying to bring back the Catholic religion?

The general opinion seemed to be that it was better just to wait. James was nearly sixty, after all. When he died, Mary would be the next ruler. Of course James was an unpleasant and rather stupid man but they wouldn't have to put up with him for long.

A William and Mary plate

Then, suddenly, everything changed. James II's second wife, Mary of Modena, gave birth to a son. As a boy, the new baby became heir to the throne over his half-sister Mary. Everyone realized that the boy would be brought up as a Catholic, like his parents.

Now there was no point in the Protestants waiting for James to die. They could see in their mind's eye a long line of Catholic kings stretching away into the future. They lost no time in sending a letter to William of Orange, inviting him to bring his army to England and drive Catholic James out. The letter was carried to Holland by Admiral Herbert, disguised as an ordinary sailor.

William began to get ready for the invasion. When James heard that William had gathered together 14,000 men and over 500 ships with which to transport them to England, he panicked. He tried to undo the mistakes he had made during his three-year reign but it was too late.

William landed at Torbay on 5 November 1688. James II's army was almost twice as big. It was marched a short distance towards the west country and made camp near Salisbury. It looked as though a tremendous battle was going to take place.

In fact, there was no battle because many of James's army leaders took their men and deserted to William. All over the country there were revolts and demonstrations against the king. James II saw that the position was hopeless and left the country. On the way, he dropped the Great Seal of England into the Thames, hoping that this would hinder the running of the country.

Both Parliament and people acclaimed Dutch William and his wife as William III and Mary II. There would never be a Catholic ruler again, nor would any future king be able to rule England as he liked. From now on king and Parliament would work together.

3 Science

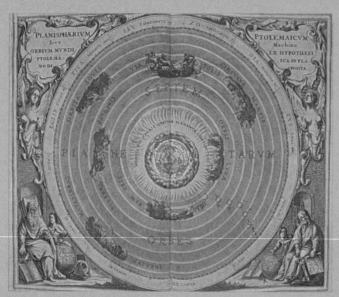

The old view of the universe with the earth in the centre

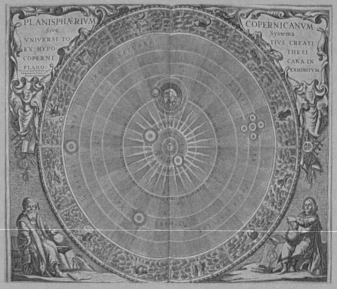

The Copernican view of the universe

Not long before the Stuart period, most educated men had believed that each planet was fixed to a huge, hollow crystal ball and that all these spheres, as they called them, revolved round the earth.

We know now that these ideas were wrong but in those days, such matters came under the heading of religion, not science. Science, as a way of getting to know what makes things work, was not yet accepted.

The universities were not interested in the scientific method. Whenever a problem arose, the official way of solving it was either to argue the thing out or to give a ruling that everyone had to accept. It never occurred to most people that it's best to get the facts right first. Copernicus and Galileo had already shown that the strange movements of the planets could be explained by accepting that the sun, and not the earth, is in the middle of the system.

The Church in those days imprisoned, or even put to death, those who said they believed in the new theories. But by the middle of the seventeenth century, quite a number of people were beginning to think it was silly to debate the truth when you could find a way of showing it. Isaac Newton explained why the moon and the planets kept travelling in circles. His very important discovery was the Law of Gravity.

One reason why people's thinking was changing was because population numbers were rising. This led to more trade and travel and more ships. The captains wanted to know how to find out where they were when they couldn't see land.

It was easy enough to measure the angle of the sun or a star above the horizon and from that to say how far north or south of the Equator you were. But there was no simple way to work out how far east or west you had

Sir Isaac Newton

Newton's reflecting telescope

travelled. However, a careful study of the moon and stars helped mathematicians to draw up tables which sailors could use.

Growing numbers of people needed more and more coal so the mines had to be dug deeper. Some of these filled with water and couldn't be worked. Several ideas were tried to get the water out of the pits but the only one that worked at all during the 1600s was Thomas Savery's 'Miner's Friend'. Before the Stuart period was over, Thomas Newcomen's steam pump was clearing some coal mines of water.

These practical things were based on an immense amount of pencil and paper work and the experiments by a new kind of man, to whom we must now give the name 'scientist'.

Charles II was very interested in science and allowed a group of thinkers to call themselves The Royal Society. They met regularly from 1662 and talked about the work they had been doing. Other members could point out where somebody had gone wrong or repeat their experiments if they wished. Something new had been learned when several men got the same results from an experiment.

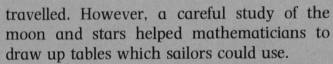

Quadrant for measuring the angle of the sun or stars

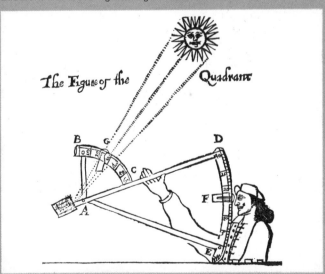

Science

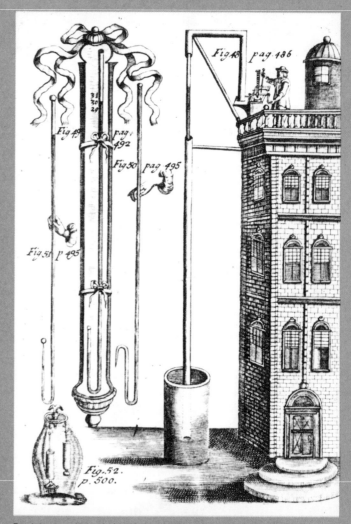

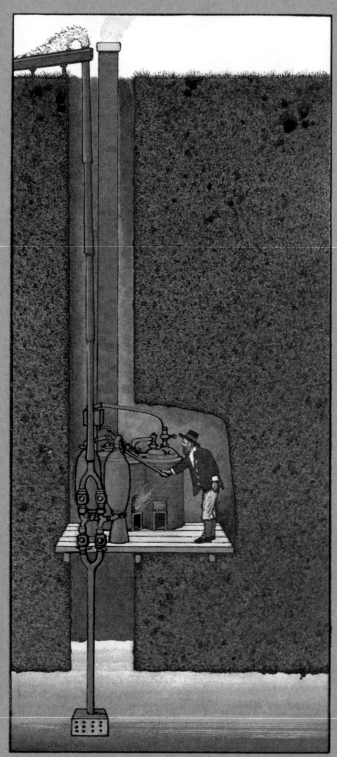

Savery's mine pump

Boyle's experiment with air pressure

above Edmund Halley
above left Halley's diving bell
above right The comet named after Halley
right Boyle's vacuum pump
far right Boyle
below Hooke's microscope

An experiment with light (Newton)

4 Law and Order

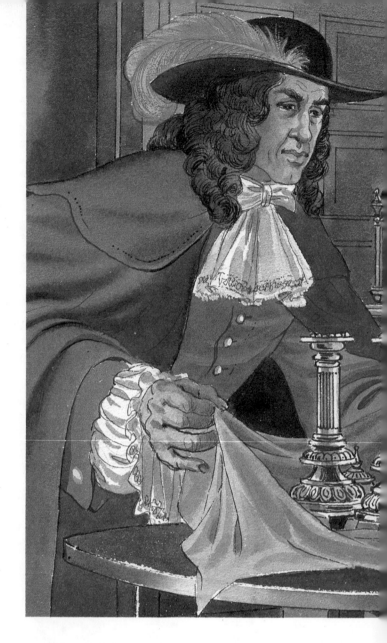

If your house is broken into and burgled, what ought you to do? The most sensible thing would be to tell the police. A detective will probably come round to look and to ask questions. If you are lucky, the thief will be caught and you might get your valuables back.

It wasn't like that in those days. Let's ask a gentleman of the early 1700s to tell us what happened when he was robbed.

'It's a long time ago now,' he says, 'and I'm not sure I can put all the details in the right order but I'll try. I came downstairs one morning about eleven or twelve years ago to find that a thief had got in during the night and stolen a pair of silver candlesticks and some other odds and ends.

'My first thought was to call in the Charlie, or watchman, but he didn't know anything and hadn't seen anything. Not surprising, really, for he was at least seventy and most of his nights were spent in his little watchman's hut. He did patrol from time to time, calling out the hour and the weather, but a criminal had only to wait for him to pass to be safe for at least an hour.

'I reported my loss to the parish constable but he held out no hope. I had no witnesses, he told me. So I resigned myself to the fact that I should never see my candlesticks again.

'Imagine my surprise when a gentleman called to see me about a week later. He had a strong, perhaps even coarse, face but dressed and spoke quietly. He offered his services as a "thief taker" and finder of stolen goods.

'He persuaded me to set a reward and made me promise not to prosecute the thief if he should be found. "It's easier like this to get

stuff back," he said. "Very well," I replied, "I agree to your terms, Mr. er – ?" "Wild. Jonathan Wild."

'I then forgot about him and my silver until three weeks later. He called, gave me my candlesticks back and claimed the reward. I was delighted and paid up. Before he left, he gave me a sheet of paper on which was printed his name and portrait, together with the address of a new office he was opening in London.

'A friend of mine went there once and a clerk took down the details of what he had lost. He, too, got his property back. I remember thinking what a good thing it was that this lawless city of London had men like Jonathan

Wild. At least there was one man fighting crime.

'Several years went by and rumours began to be heard that Wild wasn't the honest man he pretended to be. Everything came out at his trial. Far from tracking down the thief, he had actually ordered him to rob my house. Provided I promised not to lay charges against the robber, the thief was safe and so was Wild.

'What a foolproof scheme he had! Thieves all over England, let alone London, brought their loot to him and he only pretended to try and trace it, so he and his crony could split the reward money and I could get my goods back. If he couldn't return things, they were altered and perhaps sold abroad. He had no

mercy on a robber who disobeyed him or complained about his share. Wild thought nothing of turning him over to a constable with enough evidence to hang him.

'Wild himself was hanged at Tyburn in 1725 but I must say it didn't make the crime figures drop. It's still unsafe to walk the streets at night and sometimes even in daylight. Because of the highwaymen, you can almost rely on being robbed if you are upon the road.

'All the government does is to make hanging the punishment for more and more crimes but the criminals just laugh. So few of them get caught, it doesn't really sink in that they might end on the gallows.'

5 A Country Parson

Let's visit Parson Clegg at his new parsonage. The house is new but Thomas Clegg is old. He has lately come into some money after being poor most of his life and has had the old house pulled down and this new one put up in its place.

It is brick built as timber is getting scarce and expensive. Even wood for the fire is beyond the means of most of the villagers. They burn dried turf or do without.

The windows are the new sliding sashes with larger panes of glass. The windows are set in straight lines, unlike the ones in the old parsonage, which appeared here and there in the walls, seemingly without pattern.

Thomas Clegg is celebrating his seventieth birthday this very day. He is waiting for the guests who are coming to take tea with him. His wife died many years ago but his two married daughters are expected any minute. They will have their husbands and children with them.

His unmarried daughter keeps house for him. His son is an officer in the army and is away fighting with Marlborough against the French. The only other caller is Squire Johnson who rode over from the Manor House earlier in the day.

The visitors arrive and are ushered in through the front door. We'll follow them in to see what the new house looks like inside.

The hall runs through to the back of the house and is quite wide with doors opening off it on both sides. Like most of the rooms, the lower half is panelled in wood with white painted walls above. The staircase is also wide and faces the front door.

On the ground floor are the dining, drawing and sitting rooms. On the top floor are the servants' quarters, the bedrooms and the parson's study. This is where he writes his sermons and the whole room is lined with leather-backed books.

In the drawing room, the guests are served tea in china cups. Surprisingly, these have no handles. Even less to our taste, the tea is weak, with no sugar or milk. This is a new habit at the parsonage, for tea is very expensive, costing up to £2 a pound – or about six weeks' wages for a workman. The farm workers in the village can't afford tea, even those who do have jobs or strips of land to farm.

After tea, the children play in the garden; the two married sisters exchange gossip while their husbands talk about crops and the weather. Parson Clegg and the Squire stroll across the garden to the churchyard. Beyond it is the decaying tithe barn, where the villagers have to bring part of their harvest each year. A little farther off is the glebe which is the parson's own land.

The Squire is talking but Thomas has gone off into a daydream. He sees the grave of his dead wife and remembers when he met her. His own father, although a cattle dealer, had been rich enough to send Thomas to Cambridge where he took his degree. His first post was as a curate and he had met and married the vicar's daughter.

He has been master of his own parish here for nearly fifty years. He has seen governments come and go and he has managed not to upset any of them. He and his wife had seven children but three of them died young, one a baby only four months old.

The Squire is asking him about new ways of farming and what they might do for the poor. Thomas doesn't want to talk about these things and can hardly say he wasn't listening, so he thinks of something he knows will amuse his friend. 'Did you know,' he begins, 'that you can split the name "Shak-speare" into two parts, with four and six letters each. If you count 46 words from the beginning of psalm 46 and 46 from the end, a most amazing . . .' His voice fades out as the two men continue their walk.

6 Public Health

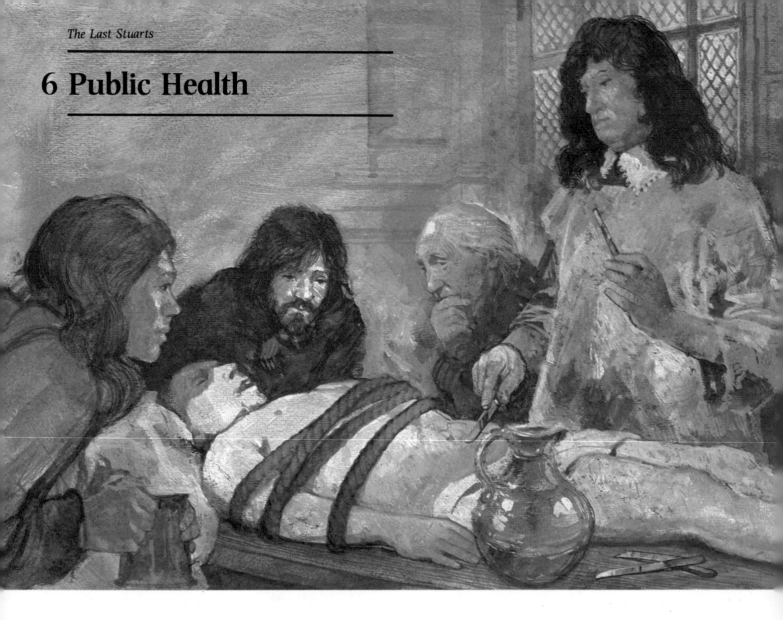

Neither William nor Mary had very long reigns. Mary died of smallpox in 1694 and William was killed in 1702. His horse stumbled on a molehill while he was out riding at Hampton Court. The couple had no children, so Mary's sister, Anne, became queen.

War had broken out between France and England at the beginning of Anne's reign. Everyone thought that France with its magnificent army would win easily but the English under John Churchill, later Duke of Marborough, won victory after victory against them. The war was to last to the end of Anne's reign.

It was a pity that men could do no better than fight each other when they might have fought against the widespread diseases of those days. The state of the people's health was extremely bad.

The Plague had almost vanished after the terrible summer of 1665 but there were plenty of other diseases. Smallpox was a killer, too. Sometimes the victim recovered but was marked or handicapped for life. Even Queen Mary II could not be saved from smallpox by her doctors. Typhus, or jail fever, also claimed many lives.

Many doctors had few, if any qualifications, had passed no exams and were simply men who were interested. The most a patient could expect was that his doctor had served some sort of apprenticeship. In fact, doctors

112

were looked upon as being no better than any other kind of craftsman.

Housewives tried to look after the health of their families with simple herbal cures and common-sense nursing but there was a good deal of ignorance and superstition. If a person had no garden or no skill in picking the right herbs, he could go to apothecaries who sold pills, potions and ointments which they made themselves.

The barber-surgeons would take out teeth and perform other simple operations, as well as shaving and cutting hair. If a leg or an arm had to come off, the patient had to be made drunk, knocked out or tied down. There was no way in those days to make him unconscious with injections or gas.

No one knew anything about germs. Even a century and a half later, when Pasteur tried to show that diseases are caused by germs, there were many people who refused to believe him.

The main reason why health was bad was the conditions in which people lived. Their drinking water came from rivers which were also used as dumps for waste. There were still no dustmen to collect rubbish from houses. Personal habits rarely included washing or taking a bath and (even in the richest families) laundry was only done once a month at best. Among the poor in the slums, clothes were scarcely washed at all.

It took more than 150 years for men and women to realize that disease starts in dirt and can then be spread to the not so dirty. What hope did ordinary people have of escaping killer diseases, when the royal family could not?

Queen Anne had no less than fifteen children, all of whom had died young. The eldest had survived only to his fourteenth year. When the queen herself passed away in 1714, the Stuart line came to an end. The next ruler was George I, a German-speaking prince from Hanover and a descendant of James I.

A modern operation

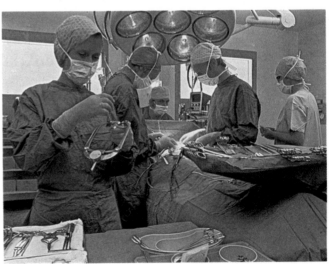

7 The Jacobite Risings

top Queen Anne
above George II

top George I
above Bonnie Prince Charlie

The two risings which happened in 1715 and 1745 are actually called the Fifteen and the Forty Five. When Queen Anne died in 1714, the throne passed to a German prince from Hanover. He and the three kings who came after him were all named George. They ruled England for over a hundred years. The Stuarts tried several times to take the crown away from them but they never managed to do so.

James II's son tried in 1715. His name was also James but his enemies called him the Old Pretender. He wasn't a very inspiring leader and didn't even land in Scotland until his cause was almost lost. Six weeks later his supporters, or Jacobites, as they were called, watched him sail away again. The Fifteen had petered out.

Thirty years on, his son, Charles Edward, made the second main attempt. This was known as the Forty Five. Charles Edward was a very different person from his father. The English dubbed him the Young Pretender but his friends knew him as Bonnie Prince Charlie, or the Young Chevalier.

He landed in the Hebrides in July 1745 with only a handful of followers. His good looks and charm soon made him many more friends. When he raised his standard in Glenfinnan, the clansmen of the Highlands flocked to join his army in large numbers.

In less than a month, Edinburgh had surrendered to the prince. Four days after its fall, the Highlanders beat an English army at Prestonpans. Everything seemed to be in the prince's favour – the English had their hands full with a war in Europe and the time seemed to be ripe for an invasion of England. Just two things were needed before they could be sure of success: some help from the French and a few thousand English volunteers from across the border.

They waited but no help came from France. Charles could delay no longer and set off for the south with 6,500 men. It was late in the year before they left and well into December by the time they reached Derby.

There were signs of panic in the capital, for the Highland army was no more than 125 miles away. Charles knew this was his last chance and wanted to press on but his advisers pointed out that this would be unwise. English soldiers had been brought back from Europe and English Jacobites had not come forward to join the Highlanders. With a heavy heart the prince gave the order to retreat.

Duke of Cumberland

Once back in Scotland, they beat off an English attack at Falkirk but could not hold Edinburgh. Finally they came up against an English army under the Duke of Cumberland, George II's son. The two armies met at Culloden near Inverness on 16 April 1746. The battle was a fierce one but the Highlanders were tired, cold and hungry, and were routed. A thousand of their dead were left on the moor after the fighting had ended.

It is easy to see why the Scots called the English general 'Butcher' Cumberland: he had the stragglers hunted down and slaughtered and even the wounded and prisoners were killed. The government in London passed laws to make sure that the old clan life of the Highlands was finished for ever.

Charles managed to get away from the moor and spent the next five months dodging the redcoat patrols. Such was the loyalty of the Scots, that not even a reward of £30,000 could tempt any of them to betray him. He finally escaped to Europe in a French ship.

Over forty years later, he died in Rome, a hopeless drunkard. Perhaps he drank to blot out the memory of all those gallant men who had died in his cause.

His younger brother, Henry, became a cardinal in the Roman Catholic church. With his death in 1807, the direct line of Stuart descent came to an end. If things had been different, he might have become Henry IX.

Bonnie Prince Charlie shortly before his death

Sweet William

Stinkwort

After the battle the English named a flower after the Duke of Cumberland. The Scots renamed a weed 'Stinking Billy'

The publishers would like to thank the following for
permission to reproduce photographs:

A – Z Collection, p.116(left and right); Ashmolean Museum,
p.8(left); Barnaby's Picture Library, p.42; BBC Copyright
Photographs, p.38; Birmingham Museums and Art Gallery, pp.54,
102; Jack Bricklebank, p.89(top left and top right); British Library,
p.11(top right); British Tourist Authority, p.99(bottom left and
bottom right); Central Office of Information, p.113(bottom right);
The City of Manchester Art Galleries, p.101(bottom); Clerk of the
Records, House of Lords, p.65; Cooper-Bridgeman Library,
pp.70(left), 97(bottom left); The Cromwell Museum, pp.63, 67,
76(left); Crown Copyright, pp.16, 17(both), 64; Fotomas Index,
pp.43, 66, 80(top), 87(top and bottom), 96(bottom left and bottom
right), 101(top), 115(top), 116/117; Michael Holford Photographs,
pp.54(top), 99(top left, top right, and top centre), 105(top right),
107(centre right and bottom left); J. T. Jackson, pp.73(left),
89(bottom); Mansell Collection, pp.45, 113(bottom left); Mary
Rose Trust, p.19(left, centre, and right); The Master and Fellows,
Magdalene College, Cambridge, p.91; Museum of London, pp.35,
76/77, 80(bottom), 90, 92/93; The National Gallery, p.96(top);
National Portrait Gallery, London, pp.13, 29, 30, 44, 50, 62,
97(top left and top right), 98(top right), 100, 105(top left), 107(top
left and centre left), 114(bottom left, bottom right, top left and top
right), 115(bottom); The National Trust, pp.98(bottom left and
bottom right), 99(centre left and right); Michael Poulton,
p.59(right); Ann Ronan Picture Library, pp.104(left and right), 105
(bottom right), 106(top right and bottom right), 107(bottom right);
Royal College of Music Museum, p.97(both bottom right); Society
of Antiquaries of London, p.36; Southwark and Lambeth
Archaeological Excavation Committee, pp.8(right), 82(both);
Jeffrey Tabberner, pp.11, 73(right); Victoria and Albert Museum,
p.6; Terry Williams, p.82(top and bottom); Woodmansterne Ltd,
pp.59(left), 81, 94.

Illustrations by Victor Ambrus, Peter Andrews, Robert Ayton,
Nicholas Brennan, Norma Burgin, Stephen Cocking, Brian Evans,
Oliver Frey, George Fryer, John Higgins, Margaret Jones, Christine
Molan, Tony Morris, Roger Payne, Trevor Ridley, and Michael
Whittlesea.

The cover illustration, by Christine Molan, shows a Sixteenth-
Century ship's boy climbing the ratlines.